Playing *Through* Arthritis

How to Conquer Pain and Enjoy Your Favorite Sports and Activities

David S. Silver, M.D.

Clinical Chief of Rheumatology, Cedars Sinai Medical Center

Contemporary Books

Chicago   New York   San Francis
Milan   New Delhi   San Juan

D0544090

Library of Congress Cataloging-in-Publication Data

Silver, David S.
 Playing through arthritis : how to conquer pain and enjoy your favorite sports and
activities / David S. Silver.
  p. cm.
 Includes bibliographical references and index.
 ISBN 0-07-140224-1
 1. Osteoarthritis—Popular works. I. Title.

RC931.067 S56 2003
616.7′223—dc21   2002031415

1 2 3 4 5 6 7 8 9 0 AGM/AGM 2 1 0 9 8 7 6 5 4 3

ISBN 0-07-140224-1

Interior design by Think Design Group
Interior illustrations by Gary Torrisi Studio

McGraw-Hill books are available at special quantity discounts to use as premiums and sales
promotions, or for use in corporate training programs. For more information, please write to the
Director of Special Sales, Professional Publishing, McGraw-Hill, Two Penn Plaza, New York, NY
10121-2298. Or contact your local bookstore.

This book is printed on acid-free paper.

*To my father, Jerry, the greatest man I have ever known.
Thanks for teaching me all that is good and making me
who I am.*

Contents

Foreword   ix

Acknowledgments   xi

Before You Begin   xiii

Introduction   1

THE FIRST QUARTER

Exercise   13

How Does Exercise Prevent and Treat Osteoarthritis?   14

Joint Flexibility and Range of Motion   17
Lower Back   18
Knees and Hips   24
Ankles and Feet   29
Neck   30
Upper Back and Shoulders   34
Elbows   39
Wrists, Hands, and Fingers   39

Muscle Strength and Endurance   41
Lower Back   41
Knees   45
Hips   50
Ankles and Feet   51
Neck, Upper Back, and Shoulders   53
Elbows   56
Wrists, Hands, and Fingers   57

Aerobic Exercise   59
Walking   61
Bicycling   62
Yoga and Tai Chi   63
Swimming   64
Other Aerobic Exercises   64

Warm Water Exercises   65

The Final Play   68

THE SECOND QUARTER

Nutrition and Vitamins 69

Ideal Body Weight and Arthritis   70

Are There Foods or Vitamins That May Help
  Prevent or Treat Arthritis?   73
  Whole Foods Versus Refined Foods   73
  Omega-3 Fatty Acids   74
  Nightshade Foods   75
  Bioflavonoids   75
  Antioxidants   76
  Vitamin A and Beta-Carotene   77
  The B Vitamins   77
  Vitamin C   78
  Vitamin D   78
  Vitamin E and Selenium   79
  Boron   79
  Zinc   80

How Much of These Vitamins and Minerals
  Should I Take?   80

The Model Arthritis Diet   81

HALFTIME PEP TALK

Coping with Stress and Depression 85

Recognizing the Signs and Triggers of Stress   87

Depression   91

THE THIRD QUARTER

Traditional Therapies 95

Acetaminophen   96

Topical Creams   97

Injections   99

Pain Medications   101

Nonsteroidal Anti-Inflammatory Drugs   102

COX-2 Inhibitors   105

Diacerein   108

Metalloproteinase Inhibitors   108

Tetracyclines   109

Heat and Cold   109

Bracing   110

Liquid Cartilage   111

Surgery   111

Is the Cure on the Horizon?   112

How Does All of This Fit into Your Strategy?   113

THE FOURTH QUARTER
Alternative Therapies   115

General Guidelines   117

Glucosamine and Chondroitin   119

MSM, SAM-e, DMSO, and Other Sulfur Compounds   122

Cetyl Myristoleate   124

Emu Oil   125

Other Herbal and Dietary Remedies   125
    Turmeric (Curcumin)   126
    Boswellia   126
    Ginger   127
    Bromelain   128
    Cartilage and Collagen   129

Acupuncture   130

Magnet Therapy   131

Massage, Rolfing, and Feldencritz   132

Manipulation and Other Manual Techniques   133

Homeopathy   134

WORKING OVERTIME
Your Personalized Arthritis Strategy   137

Step 1: Set Your Goals   138

Step 2: Make Time   139

Step 3: Figure Out What to Incorporate
into Your Strategy   141

Step 4: Choose Exercises to Meet Your Goals   142

Walking and Jogging   143
Hiking   144
Golf   144
Tennis   147
Basketball   150
Softball and Baseball   152
Soccer   154
Skiing (and Snowboarding)   155
Football   159
Volleyball   160
Bicycling   161
In-Line Skating   162
Aerobics   162
Swimming   164
Bowling   165
Other Sports   165
Sex and Arthritis   165

Step 5: Choose the Right Medication   166

Step 6: Find the Right Doctor   167

Rheumatologists   167
Orthopedic Surgeons   168
Physiatrists   168
Internists   168
Family Practitioners   169

Step 7: Put It All Together   169

Final Thoughts   171

Bibliography   173
Index   181

Foreword

I have been around athletes for most of my adult life. As owner of the Los Angeles Lakers for more than twenty years, I have had the privilege of getting to know some of the most gifted basketball players of all time, and unfortunately I have watched some go on after their careers to develop osteoarthritis. I have also seen many of my friends and family suffer the same severe joint pains as some of my former players.

Arthritis affects about 43 million Americans. Although athletes commonly develop osteoarthritis because of the wear and tear they put on their joints, all of us are at risk for contracting this debilitating disease. Whether you are a casual walker or a marathon runner, there are things you can do to either prevent the onset of osteoarthritis or reduce the symptoms once you have it.

Playing Through Arthritis lays out a comprehensive strategy to help you overcome this crippling disease and get back to doing the things you like. Exercise is the cornerstone of any successful arthritis strategy, and getting started on the right program is crucial if you want to try and prevent or treat osteoarthritis. Eating smart and healthy and maintaining your appropriate weight can help to not only improve your arthritis but also reduce your risk of heart attack and stroke. Knowing when to go to your doctor to ask about medication and being knowledgeable about the available options for treatment can help you to live with less pain. Preparing for sports, be it basketball or bowling, can help you to prevent that initial injury that can eventually lead to the development of arthritis.

Both professional and casual athletes alike are at risk for developing osteoarthritis. If you prepare and take the necessary precautions, you can continue to remain active for many years—without the pain and stiffness that osteoarthritis can cause. You can beat arthritis at its own game.

—Dr. Jerry Buss
Owner, Three-Time Defending World Champion
Los Angeles Lakers

Acknowledgments

I first and foremost want to thank my wife, love, and best friend, Michele, for her support, encouragement, and belief that I could actually do this. Without her by my side, none of this would mean anything. To my beautiful children—Dana, Michael, Scotty, and Justin—my most precious gifts, who lost countless hours with their dear old Dad during the writing of this book and who would always be there to give me a hug or a smile just when I needed it most. To my mother, brothers, sister, grandmother, and in-laws, who are always there for me.

To all of the teachers, mentors, physicians, and other health care professionals who I have learned from and continue to learn from every day: Stuart Silverman, M.D., Michael Weisman, M.D., the late James Klinenberg, M.D., David Bressler, Ph.D., Peter Weiss, M.D., Peter Waldstein, M.D., Gurkirpal Singh, M.D., and my staff. To Jonathan and Faye Kellerman for being my sounding board. To all of my patients, who are my real teachers.

To all of the others who have helped make this possible: Michael Canale, Jimmy Walsh, Jennifer and Sean Buss, and Linda Rambis. And, of course, to Dr. Jerry Buss, Joe Namath, Denise Austin, Ambassador Martha Lara, and Georges Marciano for their powerful words. To my agent, Joel Gotler, and my editors, Judith McCarthy and Susan Moore, for their guidance during this project, and to Gary Torrisi for his wonderful illustrations.

And thank G–d for all he has given me.

Before You Begin

This book is an educational tool to assist you in the prevention and treatment of osteoarthritis. It cannot and should not take the place of your physician or other qualified health care professionals in diagnosing and treating your medical problems, including osteoarthritis. The author and publisher of *Playing Through Arthritis* disclaim any responsibility if you have a reaction to any treatment described in this book, be it medication, exercise, diet, or alternative therapy. The author and publisher do not specifically endorse any product discussed in this book. Some of the treatments described may not have been approved by the FDA or any other regulatory agency, but are discussed based on the author's clinical experience and his or others' research. Use of any brand name of any product should not be construed as an endorsement of said product, nor should discussion of said product. Before you embark on any exercise regimen or diet, or take any medication, vitamin, or supplement, consult a physician or other licensed health care professional.

Introduction

The weather forecast promises a beautiful and sunny day, but you know better. Your knees begin to ache, your hands get stiff, and you know that it'll be raining before the night is over. You can't figure out how you always know when it is going to rain while the weather forecasters get it wrong. You only wish they would pay *you* that big salary to be on TV.

People are more active now than ever before. Over 100 million Americans are presently involved in exercise and athletics, including aerobics, walking, jogging, basketball, soccer, tennis, and golf, to name just a few. You may be one of the many people who have to limit their activity because of the pain and stiffness of arthritis. Or perhaps you are already active and want to avoid developing arthritis as you get older. Either way, the great news is that you can prevent and treat the pain and stiffness of arthritis.

The disease that most commonly causes achy joints in Americans is *osteoarthritis*. The name itself, though widely used, is something of a misnomer. It is derived from the root *osteo*, meaning "bone," and *arthritis*, meaning "inflammation of the joints." Osteoarthritis is not a disease of the bone until its more advanced stages, and inflammation is not a hallmark of the disease, although inflammation is involved to some degree. A term that may better describe the condition is *degenerative joint disease*.

Almost 70 million Americans suffer from arthritis. It affects both young and old, although predominantly people over the age of forty. It is estimated that by the year 2020, over 90 million people in the United States will have arthritis—that's one out of four Americans! And over 900 million people in the world suffer with arthritis. That is more than everyone with heart disease and cancer combined.

Why is arthritis so common? What causes it? What can we do about it? And why do your knees ache every time it's going to rain?

What Is Osteoarthritis?

Osteoarthritis is a disease of the joints. It has been called many things, including *degenerative arthritis, rheumatism,* and *wear-and-tear arthritis.* Most people who say they have "arthritis" actually have osteoarthritis. It has often been confused with *rheumatoid arthritis,* an inflammatory arthritis that usually affects people between the ages of twenty and forty. Rheumatoid arthritis causes severe swelling of the joints and morning stiffness, and tends to be equal on both sides of the body. It affects an estimated 2 million people in the United States, mostly women. It usually affects the small joints of the hands, but not the smallest joint (called the *distal interphalangeal joint*). Most people who come to a doctor's office thinking they have rheumatoid arthritis actually have osteoarthritis.

Osteoarthritis, in contrast, usually occurs in people over the age of forty, and is by far the most common type of arthritis. It can affect almost any joint in the body, including the distal interphalangeal joints, the first CMC joint (the joint at the base of the thumb), the spine, the hip, and the knee. It can affect joints in a sporadic fashion, and tends to be present in locations where injury has occurred. The most common symptoms are pain and stiffness. The pain of osteoarthritis is usually the most debilitating symptom. *Playing Through Arthritis* will help you to devise a game plan to beat the pain.

Many people confuse the term *osteoarthritis* with *osteoporosis.* Despite the similarities in the names, the diseases are not related. Osteoporosis is often referred to as "brittle bone disease." Patients with osteoporosis have lower bone mass and are more likely to suffer bone fractures. Osteoporosis does not involve the joints. The only apparent relation between the two diseases is that patients with osteoporosis may actually be at lower risk for developing arthritis.

Joints are everywhere in the body—not just the hands, feet, and knees, but also in the neck, chest, and back. Any of these joints can be affected by osteoarthritis. The joint is made up of several structures. It is lined with *synovium,* a membrane that provides nutrients for the joint and produces *synovial fluid* that helps to lubricate the joint. The surfaces of the joint are lined with *cartilage,* which is made mostly of water and *matrix*, a collection of *collagen* and other various molecules. (Collagen is an insoluble fibrous protein that is the primary substance in almost all structures in the body, including bones, skin, and internal organs. Collagen forms long strands of varying lengths and strengths, allowing for many of the differences we see among these structures.) The unique makeup of cartilage allows it to absorb enormous amounts of force, yet maintain stiffness and prevent injury. However, it has no blood supply or nerve endings. The cartilage depends on the synovium and the *subchondral bone* (the bone immediately underneath the cartilage) for its nutrients, leaving the cartilage susceptible to injury and impairing healing.

The development of osteoarthritis is related to damage to the cartilage and the surrounding structures. When the cartilage is injured, its cells try to self-repair by increasing production of the matrix. Unfortunately, in osteoarthritis the cells also produce enzymes called *collagenases* and *metalloproteinases* in greater amounts, leading to destruction of the cartilage. Over many years, the cartilage, which is normally extremely smooth to allow the joint to move freely and slide effortlessly thousands of times per day, begins to roughen and wear away. The synovium thickens and becomes inflamed, albeit mildly relative to other forms of arthritis. Bone spurs, or *osteophytes*, begin to form, and pain usually follows.

Without intervention, the destruction of the cartilage continues unabated and the symptoms worsen. Your back starts to creak and your hands don't work quite as well as they used to. The joints start to crack and crunch like a bowl of Rice Krispies with milk. Pain and stiffness begin to creep in and joint swelling can occur. You lose motion in the joint and it becomes deformed. You walk with a limp, can't hold a pencil; simple tasks become difficult. What you once took for granted is now a challenge.

Symptoms

The symptoms of osteoarthritis can begin quite subtly, with minimal pain and discomfort. The pain tends to worsen over time, leading to increasing difficulty performing everyday activities. The joints can swell, though the swelling tends to be mild. Patients will often perceive joints to be swollen, and sophisticated x-ray techniques will reveal subtle inflammation even if you or your doctor cannot feel it.

Because cartilage does not have nerve endings, the pain from osteoarthritis does not come from the cartilage. Instead it comes from bone spurs, synovium, and surrounding muscles, tendons, and ligaments. Although damage to and destruction of the cartilage is the primary process of osteoarthritis, it is actually the changes in all of the surrounding structures that lead to the pain you feel. This is why *Playing Through Arthritis* emphasizes the role of strength and flexibility of the joints and muscles in reducing the pain of osteoarthritis.

When the barometric pressure falls before it rains, your joints begin to expand and stretch. In the normal joint there is plenty of room for this expansion, and you do not feel it. But in the arthritic joint the damaged structures stretch, causing you to feel more pain and stiffness. A small amount of swelling also occurs, causing increased pain and decreased function.

The pain from osteoarthritis does not necessarily correlate with the findings on an x-ray. People who have severe changes on x-ray may have little if any discomfort, while patients with mild changes can have excruciating pain. The reasons for this are not well understood, but using techniques such as MRI and bone scan may provide clues. Doctors still aren't certain of all the reasons osteoarthritis causes pain—but given the enormous impact it can have on the joint and its surrounding structures, it's no surprise that it does.

You may have arthritis (as demonstrated on x-ray) and not even know it. If the changes don't cause you discomfort, do you really care? It is pain and stiffness, not x-ray findings, that lead you to limit your activity and that reduce your quality of life.

Risk Factors for Developing Osteoarthritis

Trauma to joint or
    surrounding structures
Age (over forty)
Genetic predisposition
Obesity
Female
Gout and "pseudogout"
Nerve damage (e.g., diabetes)
African American

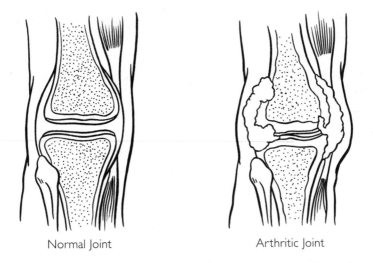

Normal Joint   Arthritic Joint

People who have one joint affected by osteoarthritis are more likely to have other joints affected. The old song that says "the knee bone's connected to the hip bone" is true. When one joint hurts, you walk differently, which puts abnormal wear and tear on other muscles and joints as they try to compensate. Damage to those other structures can lead to pain and further disability. Recognizing and attacking the disease in its earliest stages is crucial to prevent this domino effect. Preventing the disease altogether would be ideal.

Causes and Prevention

Osteoarthritis has many causes, the most common being trauma. Trauma can come in many shapes and sizes. Major injuries, such as tearing the anterior cruciate ligament of your knee during a skiing accident, can lead to large tears in the cartilage. Chronic "microdamage" can be caused by years of sitting at a computer or typewriter forty hours a week. Injuries lead to damage of the cartilage in the joint and eventually to all of the changes we see with osteoarthritis.

You can help prevent joint damage. A game plan to prevent and treat arthritis must include exercising appropriately and maintaining an ideal body weight, which are both essential for joint health. (The first two chapters of this book are devoted to these two topics.) Research has helped us to define the process of the development of osteoarthritis, starting with the initial injury to the joint. Pharmaceutical companies are actively attempting to find medications that inhibit the enzymes that lead to cartilage breakdown (the metalloproteinases and collagenases I mentioned earlier).

There are many other causes of arthritis. Genes play a significant role in the development of osteoarthritis. If your mother or father had osteoarthritis, your risk is significantly increased. Cartilage is like any other organ in the body. Some people are born with strong hearts, and some with weak hearts. The same is true for cartilage. One person may have cartilage that can withstand the rigorous activity of a stuntman, while others' cartilage can get damaged after a long walk on the beach with the wrong shoes. Doctors are still trying to understand the differences between different people's cartilage in an attempt to prevent or treat arthritis. Differences in the collagen and the way it links together may be part of the explanation, making the cartilage more susceptible to injury and, eventually, the development of arthritis.

Age is one of the strongest risk factors for the development of osteoarthritis. The reason is quite simple: the older you are, the more traumas on average you expose your joints to; the more trauma your joints suffer, the more likely your cartilage will be damaged and start to deteriorate. As our population ages, more and more people will get osteoarthritis. The aging of the baby boomers has led to an enormous growth in the number of patients with osteoarthritis. The number who suffer from osteoarthritis is expected to grow by 57 percent in the next twenty years, which has led some doctors to refer to an "osteoarthritis epidemic." Unfortunately, unless modern science changes, there isn't much doctors or anyone else can do about lowering your age.

Obesity is the most easily modified of all the risk factors for arthritis, although people presently trying to lose weight may argue with that statement. The more you weigh, the more stress is put on your joints with every movement. Increased force is transmitted to the joint, increasing the risk of joint damage. People who are overweight also tend to have weaker muscles, again leading to increased force being transmitted to the joints and causing further injury. Patients with arthritis complain that their pain prevents them from exercising, exacerbating the problem. If you have osteoarthritis and are overweight (or even if your weight is normal), exercise is crucial in preventing and improving your symptoms. Even small amounts of exercise can decrease weight, diminish pain, and improve function. When you lose weight, that force on your joints decreases, as does the pain. Appropriate dietary measures need to be instituted as part of any comprehensive arthritis treatment plan.

Women are more likely to develop osteoarthritis than are men. It is estimated that up to two-thirds of people with osteoarthritis are women. Genetic factors may contribute to the prevalence among women. The makeup of cartilage in women is slightly different than in men, which may make it more prone to injury and eventual degeneration. In addition, women on average live six to seven years longer than men. The longer you live, the more opportunity you have to damage your joints, and therefore the more likely it is that osteoarthritis will occur. Hormonal factors may play a role as well. The exact reasons are not clear, but there is no question that more women suffer from osteoarthritis than men.

Patients who have a history of *gout* or "pseudogout" appear to have an increased risk of developing osteoarthritis. Deposits of microscopic crystals in the joints cause gout and pseudogout. In the case of gout, the crystals are made up of a substance called *uric acid*, which is a normal part of the breakdown of protein and muscle. Pseudogout happens when *calcium* crystals get into joints. The crystals trigger inflammation and pain, often over a couple of hours. Patients complain of excruciating pain and swelling, and the inflammation can be so severe that it sometimes causes a fever. If inflammation persists, it can damage the cartilage and initiate or worsen the process of osteoarthritis.

Crystal disease may also worsen the symptoms of osteoarthritis once the disease is activated. Calcium crystals are more likely to get into a joint that already is arthritic, possibly worsening the disease. Studies have demonstrated that as many as 70 percent of people with osteoarthritis of the knee show evidence of crystals in the joint. The reason for this is not completely clear, but researchers continue to look at the role of these crystals in the development of arthritis and consider crystals a possible target for treatment.

People with nerve damage are more likely to develop osteoarthritis, and the group of patients most likely to have nerve damage is diabetics. Diabetes often damages nerves, resulting in numbness that usually starts in the feet and eventually travels up the legs. This numbness causes one to move in ways one shouldn't, often leading to injury—this is because the body's normal means of telling you it is being harmed (pain) is not working. One can damage the cartilage without even knowing it, often quite severely. And the damage leads to the development of arthritis. Other diseases that cause injury to the nerves, such as multiple sclerosis, can result in a similar process, but diabetes is the most common cause.

How Do You Know Whether You Have Osteoarthritis?

Your joints hurt and feel stiff, and you have been telling people for years that you have arthritis, but no one has ever actually diagnosed you with the disease. You are not alone. It is estimated that a doctor has never diagnosed arthritis in over half of the people who say they have it! The people who have been diagnosed by a doctor often do not even know what type of arthritis they have. Most people who suffer from arthritis have osteoarthritis, which is over ten times more common than rheumatoid arthritis.

Osteoarthritis is usually fairly simple to diagnose. Neither blood tests nor fancy x-rays are needed to find the disease. Patients with osteoarthritis often complain of joint pain and stiffness, and rarely of joint swelling. It becomes more difficult and uncomfortable to bend the joints, making daily activities more challenging. Consider these typical osteoarthritis patient stories.

Jane is a forty-two-year-old woman who is overall very healthy and physically active. In her early twenties she twisted her knee playing tennis. The knee swelled up for a couple of weeks, but slowly got better. Occasionally she would feel the knee catch, but she was able to play tennis and walk without significant difficulty.

About six months ago she began noticing that her knee would ache after her regular tennis match and would feel stiff and sore at night. When she got up out of a chair, the knee would hurt for a few seconds, but then feel OK. She noticed that although the knee was not swollen, it appeared slightly larger than the other, which did not give her any problems. She went to her doctor, who told her that the injury she had twenty years ago had probably torn the cartilage in the knee, causing the cartilage to wear down over the years, to the point where she now has developed osteoarthritis.

Frank is a seventy-three-year-old man who suffers from high blood pressure but is otherwise healthy. He is about forty pounds overweight and does not exercise regularly. In his fifties he began noticing that his fingers would hurt and get stiff when he typed. A couple of years later, he began noticing bumps that were sometimes painful on the ends of his fingers around the joint, and also noted pain at the base of his thumb. When he did yard work, his back would hurt and he would have to stop after about an hour and take ibuprofen. He then could continue his activities.

Over the past couple of years, the pain has gradually worsened and now includes his knees. He is unable to garden unless he takes medication first, and even then he has to quit after about thirty minutes. He is not able to pick up his grandchildren because his back and hands hurt too much. Sleep is becoming more difficult as the pain increases, and there are more bumps on his hand joints.

Many people experience the symptoms of osteoarthritis years after the initial injury, as in Jane's case, and not all people with arthritis can point to a particular injury where the symptoms were first noted.

Pain is the hallmark sign of osteoarthritis and is by far the most important. Pain is the symptom that limits you from playing sports, doing housework, opening a jar, or getting down on the floor with your children or grandchildren. People describe the pain as "achy" or "sore," although it can be sharp with certain activities or motions. The pain can be present in almost any joint, from the fingers, hands, and feet, to the knees, hips, shoulders, neck, back, or even the jaw. The pain may be constant if the disease is severe, or may come and go. The pain may travel from one joint to another, or may affect many joints at the same time. Damp or rainy weather tends to increase the pain because of decreases in the barometric pressure in the atmosphere.

People may also complain of stiffness of the joints, with or without pain. The roughening of the surface of the cartilage and

Signs and Symptoms of Osteoarthritis

Pain
Stiffness
Enlargement of joints
Lumps on joints
Mild swelling

the development of bony spurs (osteophytes) can cause the joint not to move as freely. The joint may also contain fluid or swelling, making it more difficult to move. As arthritis progresses, the joint may lose its flexibility. Its range of motion is decreased, further limiting function. Although pain is usually the most limiting factor, stiffness can prevent you from doing many of your usual activities.

As osteoarthritis progresses, the joint may not only begin to feel different, but may look different as well. Lumps can appear on the small joints of the hands rather quickly, over a period of months. The lumps can be painful, but often do not hurt. These are called *Heberdon's* or *Bouchard's nodes*, and they are a sign of osteoarthritis. The joints in other areas may become deformed and look very abnormal, especially as the disease advances. These deformities can cause pain and loss of function, but in some people they cause few problems, if any.

Although inflammation is part of the process of osteoarthritis, it is rare to see a severely swollen joint. Mild amounts of swelling are not uncommon. The swelling seen in patients with osteoarthritis usually occurs after some sort of injury or marked increase in activity. Deposits of calcium crystals can also lead to joint swelling. If multiple joints are swollen on a regular basis, you should see your doctor—something else may be going on.

The diagnosis of osteoarthritis is usually made based on your symptoms. No blood tests are available at this time that can tell you whether you have osteoarthritis, though often doctors use blood tests to rule out other diseases that might look like osteoarthritis but should be treated differently. X-rays can help confirm the diagnosis, and certain classic findings will help solidify the diagnosis. Doctors will often use x-ray to help stage the disease, although the severity of the disease on x-ray does not necessarily correlate with the severity of the symptoms you might feel. Occasionally doctors do MRIs or other sophisticated scanning techniques to confirm the diagnosis, especially if surgery is a consideration.

How Can You Win the War Against Osteoarthritis?

The reason half of all people with osteoarthritis do not see a doctor is simple: many of them feel that there is nothing that can be done about arthritis, that they are doomed to a life of pain and misery that grows more intolerable as the years wane. *Nothing could be further from the truth.* Living with pain from osteoarthritis is not inevitable. In fact, you now have the tools to overcome osteoarthritis and live an active life with little or no pain.

The goal of *Playing Through Arthritis* is to show you how you can overcome the pain and stiffness of osteoarthritis, often without the need for medication. This book will also show you ways to prevent arthritis before it has a chance to start. It is divided into four *quarters* that cover the four major steps to prevent the development and reduce the symptoms of arthritis: *exercise, diet, traditional medicine,* and *alternative therapies.*

"The First Quarter" is devoted to exercise. An appropriate work-out regimen will help you, whether you are an eighteen-year-old competitive athlete who wants to prevent the initial injury that can trigger the process of arthritis or an eighty-year-old with advanced arthritis who wants to become active again. Exercises for general conditioning and joint protection will be reviewed, as well as joint-specific exercises to help improve symptoms and function in a joint that has already been injured or is arthritic. Diagrams will instruct you in the basic exercise techniques, and you will learn how to develop a plan for putting a daily routine into place.

"The Second Quarter" explores the importance of maintaining a healthy weight. Even if you are active, obesity can cause or worsen the symptoms of arthritis. Appropriate weight reduction strategies will be discussed. A review of foods that have been touted to reduce inflammation will also be included, and you will develop a "model" arthritis diet.

"The Third Quarter" discusses the medications presently available to treat osteoarthritis. This discussion includes older medications and newer, safer, more effective alternatives. It includes a dialogue on the state of research and outlines what can be expected in the near future to help combat this disease, including some options that may eventually help you to regrow cartilage.

"The Fourth Quarter" is devoted to alternative therapies. A thorough review of glucosamine and chondroitin, MSM, SAM-e, and some lesser-known agents is included. You'll learn appropriate dosing and duration of therapies, and discover what you should watch out for when purchasing alternative agents (what you see is not always what you get).

"Working Overtime" will discuss the development of your strategy to win the war over arthritis. This section will help you to understand the importance of self-management of your disease. You will be guided on how to use the tools the book has provided to help you to beat this disease with a combination of the techniques outlined. Individual sections concentrate on how a variety of sports and leisure activities can be part of a focused fitness plan for athletes and nonathletes alike. Specific regimens for people already active in sports who want to prevent injury will be discussed. If you already suffer from arthritis, you will learn how to return to a higher level of function and to the activities that you enjoy.

The battle over your arthritis is far from hopeless. With the help of *Playing Through Arthritis*, you can win the war over the pain and stiffness of arthritis and live a fulfilling and active life.

Exercise

You have finally decided you won't put up with the pain anymore. You have been suffering for months or years with joint pain, but always thought there was nothing you could do about it. You've seen your mother or father, after an active and fulfilling life, now suffering with the debilitating pain of arthritis. Now, you realize there is something you can do about it.

"The First Quarter" is devoted to exercise, the most important thing *you* can do to overcome the pain and stiffness of osteoarthritis and, possibly, prevent it from ever occurring. It's probably no surprise to you that exercise can help, although the reasons may not make sense at first glance. Your friends, family, and doctor have been telling you for years that exercise is essential to max-

Health Benefits of Exercise

Prevents heart disease
Prevents stroke
Reduces total cholesterol
    and increases
    "good" cholesterol
Reduces blood pressure
Prevents or limits diabetes
Prevents or improves
    osteoporosis
Facilitates weight reduction
Prevents certain types of
    cancer (possibly)
Reduces depression and
    anxiety

imize the health of your heart, to lower your cholesterol, and simply to live a longer and healthier life.

You keep promising yourself that you are going to start, but you always have an excuse (work, family, the dog ate my exercise tape, and so on). Well, it is time for the excuses to end.

How Does Exercise Prevent and Treat Osteoarthritis?

As you know, osteoarthritis is a disease of the joints—specifically, the cartilage in the joints. How can exercise increase the amount of cartilage you have in your joints or heal the cartilage that's there? Until recently, there was no evidence that it could. It now appears that the right amount of the right exercise may stimulate cartilage to regrow, although this theory is far from proven. If it can't, how can exercise help you win the war against osteoarthritis?

When joints move, muscles, tendons, and ligaments control the movement. All the structures move in unison, allowing for free and easy motion. When a joint develops osteoarthritis, the joint is moved less and in a narrower range. This causes muscles to become weaker and lose their flexibility. As the muscles get weaker, the joint is exposed to greater forces and the muscles are less able to absorb the shock. The joint is more prone to damage and hurts more as you use it. A negative feedback cycle is set up, and the pain and arthritis worsen. The pain causes you to avoid exercise and the symptoms continue to escalate.

The most obvious example of this is the knee. Numerous studies have shown that the amount of damage to the knee caused by arthritis, as indicated on x-ray, does not accurately indicate a patient's pain level. What does predict the amount of pain is the strength of the quadriceps muscle. The quadriceps muscle is the muscle in the front part of the thigh. It is the muscle responsible for slowing the leg down against gravity as you go to plant your foot while walking. When the quadriceps is weak, the foot hits the ground with a greater force and the force is transmitted to the knee. If the knee already has some cartilage damage, even minor, pain can result, as well as further injury. Even if there is no damage to the joint, the increased force can lead to microinjury and begin the arthritic process.

On the contrary, let's assume your quadriceps muscles are good and strong. When you start to walk, your foot hits the ground with less force, and less force is transmitted to the knee. Injury is less likely to occur. Also, if you already have arthritis in the knee, less force means less pain, allowing you to walk farther and faster. In fact, studies have shown that if patients with arthritis go through a quadriceps strengthening program, they can reduce the pain from their osteoarthritis by 40 to 50 percent in just six weeks! And that reduction does not come as a result of a change in your cartilage. Over the long term, it is hoped that the loss of cartilage is retarded and function continues to improve. In addition, by maintaining strong quadriceps and other muscles, you may be able to *prevent* the development of osteoarthritis in the first place.

Exercises also help replenish synovial fluid, the joint's natural lubricant. When you are inactive and have osteoarthritis, the body manufactures less synovial fluid, making it more difficult to move the joint,

Walking with Force to the Knee

as it is lacking lubrication. Exercise stimulates the formation of synovial fluid and increases joint lubrication, allowing the joint to move more freely and with less pain.

In order for exercise to prevent osteoarthritis or reduce its symptoms, stretching and loosening up the muscles and ligaments is essential. When a muscle group around a joint is tight, the joint is not able to move as freely. Joints and muscles are more prone to damage at the far ends of the range of motion, leading to injury and pain and again setting a negative feedback loop into motion. Additionally, people with osteoarthritis are more prone to muscle spasms, which can cause additional discomfort. Appropriate stretching and range-of-motion exercises are essential to overcoming the pain and stiffness of osteoarthritis.

How do you know which exercises are right for you? The answer is not always simple. Often, exercise can cause discomfort when you begin—but it should *not* cause severe pain. If you are having severe pain when you do a particular exercise, stop doing that exercise. Before starting any exercise program, discuss it with your doctor, especially if you have high blood pressure or problems with your heart or lungs. Very few people are not physically capable of doing some sort of exercise, especially the ones outlined in this chapter.

Use this chapter to design the exercise program that is right for you. It includes general conditioning exercises applicable to all people, as well as exercises to reduce symptoms or prevent arthritis in particular joints. It also reviews the types of exercises available and explains why a combination of the types of exercises is essential for joint and general health.

If you have not been physically active for a long time, take care not to overdo it. One rule is to start low and go slow. If it hurts too much, you are not likely to keep doing it. If you are able to walk only one block, then walk only one block. It is still significantly better than walking

Types of General Exercise

Joint flexibility and range of motion
Muscle strength and endurance
Aerobic exercise
Warm water exercises

zero blocks. Every week you can slowly increase the amount of the activity you are doing, and before you know it you will be walking a full mile or two. It sounds easy, and it is. The toughest part is getting started and making exercise part of your daily routine.

One of the keys to getting yourself started with exercise is to choose an activity or exercise you enjoy. Although this section will outline the so-called "ideal" graduated exercise program, finding something you like and can do without a lot of pain is the best way to get started. For instance, if you enjoy swimming, water exercises or water aerobics classes may be best for you. If you like going to the gym and taking aerobic classes, an appropriate exercise class geared toward your level of physical function might be best—at least going to the gym and using the mats for your exercises might be a good place to start. Regardless of what exercise it is, if you enjoy it and it does not cause you too much pain, you are more likely to stick with it and make it a regular part of your daily routine. As you start to feel better and increase your activity level, the positive effects—diminished pain and stiffness—will give you further incentive to continue exercising. You will look and feel better, and your mood will improve as well.

None of the exercises described in this section require fancy equipment or major expense. You do not need to sign up at the most expensive health club (unless you want to) or buy $5,000 worth of weight training equipment. You may need a chair, a towel, or a flat surface to lie on, but nothing more expensive than that. Even the exercises to improve strength do not require a weight room.

No more excuses. It's time for training camp to begin.

Joint Flexibility and Range of Motion

Some people refer to these types of exercises as *stretching exercises*. One of the main factors leading to injury and triggering the process of osteoarthritis is lack of mobility. When muscles, tendons, and joints are not sufficiently stretched out, they are more prone to injury. That is why you always see professional and student athletes "loosen up" prior to a competition. For the average casual athlete who jogs or plays softball, joint flexibility and range-of-motion exercises can be crucial in preventing injury. And preventing the damage to the cartilage that ensues from injury is still the best way to prevent osteoarthritis.

Why does stretching prevent injury and osteoarthritis? When muscles and tendons are stretched, they are less likely to be "pulled." In addition, your joints move more freely. When muscles are tight, the joint moves less easily and is more likely to be injured. And if you injure a muscle, tendon, or ligament around a joint it will add more stress to the joint, making damage more likely. Loosening muscles and ligaments is like stretching a rubber band. If you stretch it too quickly it can break, but if you stretch it slowly it is able to withstand much greater forces.

Once you have osteoarthritis, you develop stiffness in the muscles and joints. You start to lose range of motion and flexibility, and this further contributes to the pain. When the pain intensifies, your muscles tighten up and restrict your motion even further. Stretching your muscles and joints enables them to move more freely and therefore with less pain. Soon you're able to do more with less stiffness and discomfort.

Some of the following exercises may be difficult when you start. Mild discomfort is common when you begin to exercise, especially if you haven't exercised for a long time or your arthritis is severe. If a particular exercise causes significant pain, stop doing it. The exercise may be too strenuous for your level of fitness or arthritis, or you may be doing the exercise incorrectly. The pain is telling you that something is wrong: listen to your body. It might help to have someone else observe you performing the movement to make sure you are executing correctly. You may be able to return to that exercise once you are in better shape.

Lower Back

The lower back is one of the most common areas where pain and stiffness are felt. From the seventeen-year-old varsity volleyball player to the eighty-year-old retired truck driver who used to bowl and play softball on the weekends, almost everyone complains of lower-back pain at some time. It is estimated that in the year 2000, over *one billion* people in the world experienced back pain. A simple regimen of exercise can greatly reduce the pain and stiffness in the back related to osteoarthritis, or prevent the injury that can trigger the process.

Joe is a twenty-seven-year-old accountant who spends the majority of his time sitting behind his desk. He likes to play softball on weekends and sometimes plays racquetball during the week. One day, while swinging his softball bat he noticed a twinge in his lower back, which developed into severe pain over the next couple of days. He started on a program of gentle stretching and strengthening with the exercises described on pages 20–22. He began to notice improvement almost immediately: decreased pain and increased flexibility. After a few weeks the pain disappeared, but Joe continued to do many of the exercises. He began noticing that his range of motion was improving and he was able to reach better in the field and move better on the racquetball court without pain or discomfort.

Helen is a seventy-two-year-old retired physician who was physically active on and off throughout her life. About five years ago she began noticing pain and stiffness in her lower back when she had been sitting too long. The pain would diminish when she stood and loosened up. Over time the pain gradually got worse and became more constant; she could stand or walk for only about five minutes and was waking up at least two times a night. She went to see an orthopedist, who told her that she had arthritis in the spine and prescribed Motrin. She came to see me and I recommended that she start a series of exercises like those outlined here. Within a few weeks she began sleeping better with less discomfort. Her standing and walking tolerance gradually increased, and she can now walk almost a mile without significant pain. Sitting is still difficult, but as long as she stands up and stretches about every fifteen minutes, she can manage reasonably well.

The majority of exercises for the lower back are done while lying on the floor, although a number of them may be done while sitting in a chair or standing up if you have difficulty getting up and down off the floor. If your mattress is very firm and your mobility is extremely limited, you can even try some of these exercises while lying in bed. Many of the exercises used to stretch out the back also stretch the abdominal muscles. The abdominal muscles can absorb much of the force that is placed on the lower back, especially when lifting or doing activities. Stretching and strengthening the abdominal muscles is critical in preventing or reducing lower-back pain. These exercises are also very helpful if you play sports that involve significant strain on the lower back, including golf, basketball, baseball, and tennis.

Stretching Exercises for the Lower Back

1. **Knee-to-Chest Pull.** Lie flat on your back with your legs straight. Pull your right knee to your chest while keeping your left leg straight. Hold your right knee for three seconds or longer, then relax. Repeat, this time bending the left knee and keeping the right straight. Try to do this five times or more. After you are in a little better shape, you can also do this exercise while pulling both knees to your chest at the same time.

2. **Pelvic Tilt.** Lie on your back with your knees bent and your feet flat on the floor. Put your arms at your sides, tighten the muscles of your abdomen and buttocks, and straighten the lower back.

Slowly raise the lower back and buttocks off the floor and hold for at least three seconds, then return them to the ground. Push your back into the ground and hold for three seconds or more before relaxing. Repeat five times or more.

3. **Leg Crossover.** Lie on your back with your arms at your sides. Bend one leg and cross it over the other, placing the foot of the bent leg flat on the ground. Rotate the hip and lower back across your body, feeling the stretch in your lower back. Do not over-stretch. Repeat five times on each side of the body.

4. **Leg Elevation.** Lie on your back with your knees bent and your arms at your sides. Raise your right leg as high as you can and try to straighten it without overstretching. Repeat with the other leg. Complete five repetitions on both sides. If you are unable to straighten the leg due to pain, keep the knee slightly bent.

5. **Chair Lower-Back Flexion.** Sit on a chair with your feet apart. Bend forward as far as you can with your arms reaching toward the floor between your knees. Touch the floor if you can. Repeat five times, trying to bend a little farther each time. Try to repeat

two to three times a day. Each time prior to doing this exercise, be sure you have done the knee-to-chest pull (see page 20).

6. **Mini-Pushup.** Lie flat on your stomach and relax as much as possible. Put your arms at your sides with your elbows bent and your hands flat on the floor. Straighten your arms and push up the top half of your body as much as you can without causing pain. Leave the lower half of your body on the ground. Hold for one to two seconds and slowly lower yourself back to the ground. If this is too difficult, place your forearms and hands flat on the floor instead and push up the top half of your body that way. This extends the back less and creates less tension. If you still have pain while lying on the floor, move your hips away from the side that has more pain and try the exercise again. Do five to ten repetitions. Do this exercise more than once a day, if possible.

7. **Wall Lunge.** Stand with your hands against the wall. Keep your abdominal and lower-back muscles tight. Keeping your feet flat on the floor, put one leg behind you with the knee straight and the other leg in front of you with the knee slightly bent. Bend forward until you feel a stretch in the back of the straight leg, then hold the position for about three seconds. Repeat five times and switch legs.

When you have mastered these exercises, you can progress by adding a strengthening program to your stretching regimen. Such a program will be described in the next section. You can begin adding strengthening exercises early on by trying one or two strengthening exercises along with your stretching routine. Over time, you can increase the number of strengthening exercises you do, and you will be amazed how quickly you can progress.

Doing all the stretching exercises just described should take only about five to ten minutes. After doing these exercises for a while, you will begin to notice decreased stiffness and increased range of motion in your back. These exercises will not only help if you already suffer from pain and stiffness in your back, but can also prevent them from occurring in the first place. The exercises can be done in a modified form prior to starting any other sports or exercise program.

Maintaining appropriate posture while sitting and standing is essential to preventing and reducing pain and stiffness in the lower back. The lower back has a natural inward curve that must be maintained when you sit, especially if you need to sit for long periods of time. Many of us tend to slouch when we are sitting, reversing the natural or normal curve of the lower back. Over time this puts increased stress and strain on the joints and muscles of the lower back, eventually leading to wear and tear on the cartilage and arthritis. Proper sitting technique will promote healthy joints in the spine and improve flexibility and mobility.

Ergonomically designed chairs that promote appropriate positioning of the lower back can be helpful but may be expensive. A simpler and less expensive way to save your back is to buy an inexpensive lumbar roll for your chair or car. A rolled-up towel may help as well but can be uncomfortable.

If you have a job that requires sitting for long periods of time, it is important that you get up to stretch for a few seconds on a regular basis. When you sit for too long, your muscles begin to tighten up and you lose good posture. This leads to pain in the back and wear and tear on the joints. Try to get up every thirty to sixty minutes to loosen up.

When you are lifting, especially lifting heavy objects, avoiding injury is crucial. By accentuating the natural curve of your lower back and not bending at the waist, you can prevent a severe problem. Keeping the object close to your body and bending at the knees is essential.

Don't be afraid to ask for help if you need it. Many back problems are created when you try to pick up something that you shouldn't.

Knees and Hips

Stretching exercises for the knee primarily involve the muscles of the thigh. The two major groups involved are the quadriceps (front thigh muscles) and the hamstrings (back thigh muscles). The quadriceps is crucial to protecting the knee against the development of arthritis. However, hamstring "pulls" are much more common than injuries to the quadriceps. Injury to either of these muscle groups can increase stress and strain on the knee joint and elevate the risk of injury. In addition, these muscles are involved in the movement of the hip joint and therefore are critical in protecting that joint as well.

The muscles of the buttocks also stabilize the hip joint. These muscles need to work in unison to prevent injury and assure free and easy motion. In addition, when you have damage to the knee joint, the risk of developing arthritis in the hip greatly increases, and vice versa. Therefore, an appropriate stretching regimen will involve both of these joints at the same time.

Jackie is a fifty-three-year-old who loves to bicycle and do yoga. She used to work out on a regular basis, but she stopped exercising for two years. She decided to take up jogging, but about two weeks into her morning jog she noticed tightness in the back of her leg. She stopped working out for a couple of weeks and got some relief, but when she tried to start again the symptoms returned. She remembered from yoga that she had been OK as long as she continued her stretching exercises. She began a program of five to ten minutes of stretching prior to jogging and was able to return without great difficulty. She is now up to three miles a day two to three days a week, and her thigh pain has not returned.

A set of simple stretching exercises can help prevent injuries to the knee and eventually allow progression to a strengthening program. Some of the exercises may result in increased muscle strength, which is an obvious bonus.

Stretching Exercises for the Knees and Hips

1. **Knee-to-Chest Pull.** (See illustration on page 20.) Lie flat on your back and pull your right knee to your chest while straightening your left leg. Hold the right knee for three seconds or longer, then relax. Repeat with the other leg. Try to do this five times or more with each leg. After you are in better shape you can try pulling both knees to the chest at the same time.

2. **Ankle Circles.** Lie flat on the ground with your legs straight. Point your toes upward toward your knees and move your ankles in a circle. This will loosen the muscle in the lower leg called the *gastrocnemius*. Repeat ten times.

3. **Hamstring Pull.** Lie flat on your back with one leg bent. Straighten your other leg and pull it toward your head. If this is difficult, put a towel around your foot and use it to pull your leg, as shown in the drawing. You should feel a pull in the back of your leg (hamstrings). Hold the position for ten seconds, then bend your knee and lower the leg to the floor. Repeat three to five times. Repeat the sequence with the other leg—again, three to five times. If the leg muscle feels too tight, don't overstretch. Loosen your hold on the leg. After a while you should be able to pull the leg farther and/or hold it for a longer period of time.

4. **Crossover Hamstring Pull.** Lie on your back with both knees bent. Cross your left leg over your right and pull your right leg

toward your chest. Hold for five seconds and return to the starting position. You should feel a pull in your hamstrings on the right and the outer aspect of your thigh on the left thigh. Repeat three to five times, then switch to the other leg.

5. **Quadriceps Pull.** Lie on your left side with both knees bent. Hold the upper part of your right foot and push it back toward your buttocks slowly so that you are increasing the bend in your leg. You should feel a stretch in the front of your thigh (the quadriceps). Hold for five seconds and release slowly. Repeat five times, then roll over to the right side and repeat.

6. **Sitting Butterfly.** Sit on the floor with your legs spread apart and the soles of your feet together. Slowly push your knees toward the floor; when you feel the stretch, hold for three to five seconds. Repeat ten times.

7. **Rolling Outer Thigh (Hip Abductor) Stretch.** Lie on your back with both of your knees bent and your feet side by side, soles flat

on the floor. Gently roll your hips to one side, trying to touch your knee to the floor. Keep your feet and legs together, and keep your shoulders firmly on the floor (it might help to look in the direction of the shoulder opposite your knees). When your knee is on the floor, hold the position for three seconds. Return to the starting position, then repeat the motion on your other side. You should feel a pull on the outer part of your upper thigh and hip. Repeat ten times. As you become more advanced, you can use your abdominal muscles to lift your knees toward your chest before rolling the hips.

8. **Table Quadriceps Stretch.** Lie down with your back on a low, steady bench or table and your knees bent so that your feet are touching the floor. Grab one knee with your hands and pull it toward your chest as far as possible. Keep the thigh of your other leg pushed flat against the table. You should feel a pull in the back of your thigh and in the front of your hip joint. Repeat with the other leg. Perform five to ten times per leg.

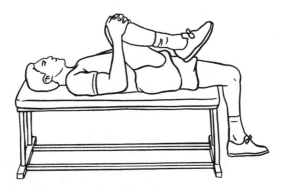

9. **Lying Butterfly.** Lie on your back with both of your knees bent. Allow your legs to separate gently while keeping your feet together. You should feel a pull on the inside of your thigh. Hold for three to five seconds, then return to the starting position. Repeat ten times.

10. **Lying Scissors Stretch.** Lie on your back with your legs straight out. Spread your legs apart as far as you can. Bring them back together. Repeat ten times.

11. **Straight-Leg Hip Rotation.** Lie on your back with your right leg bent and your right foot on the ground. Keep your left leg straight on the ground and point your left foot straight up to the sky, keeping the left knee locked. Rotate your hips from one side to another by moving your bent knee toward your straight leg while keeping the left leg on the ground. Do ten repetitions, then repeat with the right leg out straight and the left leg bent.

12. **Standing Straight-Leg Kick.** Hold on to the back of a chair with your left hand as your left side faces the chair. Bend your right leg at the knee and lift it as high as you can. Return it to the floor. Do the same with the left leg. Repeat three times. Face the other side, put your right hand on the chair, and repeat the exercise three times.

Once you have mastered these exercises you should be able to do some of the strength exercises later in this section. By maintaining good flexibility in the hip and knee, and by improving muscle tone around these joints, you can go a long way toward reducing or preventing the debilitating pain of osteoarthritis.

Ankles and Feet

Osteoarthritis does not affect the ankles as often as some of the other joints in the body, although you may find yourself at increased risk if you have had a previous fracture or numerous ankle sprains. Arthritis in the foot is much more common; because the ankles and feet need to work in unison to function optimally, the stretching exercises for these joints are considered together. The ankles and feet are constantly under pressure, bearing the weight of your entire body whenever you walk or run, so keeping them in good shape is critical.

Stretching Exercises for the Ankles and Feet

1. **Ankle Circles.** Either lying down or sitting on a chair, lift your feet off the floor and rotate your ankles, first clockwise and then counterclockwise. Repeat ten times. Next, bend your ankles to the left, then the right. Repeat ten times. Then point your toes to the sky and straighten your knees as best you can. Repeat ten times.

2. **Toe Flexion.** Either lying down or sitting on a chair, curl your toes under and then straighten them out. Repeat ten times. Spread your toes apart and bring them back together. Repeat ten times.

3. **Manual Toe and Ankle Stretch.** Take your hand and move each one of your toes and your ankles through all directions of motion.

4. **Sitting Heel Lift.** Sit in a chair and place your feet flat on the floor. Raise your heels off the floor as far as you can while keeping your toes on the floor. Put your heels back down on the floor. Repeat five times.

5. **Standing Heel Lift (Achilles Stretch).** Stand with both of your hands braced on a wall with your left leg bent at the knee and the left foot flat on the floor. Place your right leg straight out behind you with your heel off the ground. Keeping your right knee straight, slowly lower your right heel back down to the ground and hold. You should feel a stretch in the Achilles tendon (the tendon in the back of the leg just above the heel). Repeat five times. Switch legs, repeating the motion five times with the left leg.

These exercises should help to improve the motion of your feet, allowing you to walk, run, or bike with less discomfort and pain.

Neck

Most of us have experienced a stiff neck on occasion, especially if we spend a lot of time reading or working at the computer. Many people also notice stiffness in the neck when they are under stress. When the muscles in the neck spasm, the natural curve of the neck is straightened. This puts additional stress and strain on the ligaments and joints of the cervical spine. Over time, the ligaments are damaged and wear and tear is transferred to the joints, leading to injury and damage.

When arthritic changes occur in a neck joint called the *facet joint*, the joint narrows and bony spurs form. The joint lies extremely close to where the nerves coming out of the spine are located, and if spurs develop they can irritate or compress the nerves, markedly increasing the pain and creating a plethora of neurological symptoms, including pain down the arms, weakness, and numbness.

> Bonnie is a fifty-one-year-old administrative assistant who spends most of her day answering phones and doing computer work. Her work station is not ideally ergonomically designed, and she often has to twist her neck when she answers the phone or when she needs to review files while typing. About seven years ago she began noticing occasional neck stiffness at work that would resolve after she left work. Over six months, the pain began to occur on a daily basis, with occasional symptoms of pain and numbness in her right arm and hand. At times the pain would wake her up at night. She is somewhat overweight, and although she was aware that she needed to exercise, she was reluctant to start for fear that it might exacerbate her pain.
>
> Bonnie began a program of gentle neck stretches, including some she could do at work. Her pain has gradually diminished over the past several weeks. Although she still notes some discomfort, the pain no longer wakes her up at night. She walks twice a week with some of her friends and has adopted healthier eating habits.

Neck exercises can be done at home, on your commute, or even at your work desk. If your work requires frequent bending and twisting of the neck, frequent repetitions throughout the day are crucial in preventing arthritis from occurring and allowing you to remain active and pain free.

Stretching Exercises for the Neck

1. **Neck (Cervical) Rotation.** Turn your head to the left without moving your shoulders or lower body. Turn your head as far as you can without causing significant discomfort. Hold for three

to five seconds, then turn your head to the right. Hold again for three to five seconds.

2. **Chin-to-Collarbone Stretch (Sterno Stretch).** Turn your head to the left and lower your chin to your collarbone (*clavicle*). Hold for five seconds, then repeat on the right. Complete five repetitions. This will stretch your sternocleidomastoid, which runs from behind your ear to your clavicle (collarbone) and your sternum.

3. **Neck (Cervical) Extension.** Turn your head to the left and tilt it backward. Hold for three to five seconds and bring your head forward to the neutral position. Turn your head to the right and tilt the head backward. Hold again for three to five seconds. Repeat the cycle five times.

4. **Lateral Neck Pull.** Reach your right arm over your head and place your right hand against your left ear. Pull your head toward your right shoulder while resisting slightly. While your head is

tilted, turn your chin from one side to another. Relax and repeat on the other side. Complete five repetitions.

5. **Locked-Hand Neck Flexion.** Lock your hands behind your head with your elbows out to the sides and flex your neck forward without pulling or pushing on your neck. Hold for five to ten seconds. You should feel a stretch in the back of your neck and the upper part of your back. Repeat five times.

6. **Full Neck Circles.** Stretch your chin to your chest. Rotate the neck in one direction in a full circle and repeat in the other direction. (If you have neck or circulation problems, you should do only half circles.) Complete five repetitions, but be careful not to get dizzy. This exercise can be done in a sitting or a standing position.

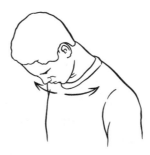

7. **Swaying Neck Extension.** Gently tip your head back and slowly rock your head from side to side. Return your head to the normal position. Repeat five times. If you develop pain in one of your arms, stop immediately. This can be a sign of nerve compression. Do not do this exercise if you get dizzy when tipping your head back.

8. **Eye Closure.** Close your eyes, then open them as wide as you can. Repeat ten times.

9. **Posterior Arm Grab.** Stand and grab your left arm with your right hand behind your back just above the wrist. Gently pull

down on your left arm while leaning your head toward the right until you feel a stretching sensation. Move your head forward and backward for a couple of seconds, then release. Repeat five times, then do the motion again on the other side, repeating five times.

Neck exercises can be done as many times a day as necessary. If you simply are using the exercises to loosen up before hitting a few golf balls or playing some hoops, then once or twice a day may be sufficient. However, if you work a desk job, you may have to get up every one to two hours to stretch and prevent damage or injury.

Neck problems can not only lead to arthritis in the neck but can trigger severe headaches as well. A regular routine of neck exercises can markedly reduce many types of headaches from muscle spasms and stress and should be included in any comprehensive program to reduce or eliminate headaches.

Upper Back and Shoulders

People who are prone to the development of neck pain or who already suffer from arthritis in the neck also commonly experience upper-back and shoulder pain. Exercises to relax the upper back and shoulders are crucial to prevent problems in the neck as well, and should be included in any comprehensive program to prevent or treat arthritis in the neck.

People with arthritis in the neck are more prone to developing arthritis in the upper back as well. Remember, the body does not work in isolated parts, but in unison. Muscles and joints work best when all parts move in harmony in one fluid motion. When one part of the body is damaged by arthritis, the surrounding areas that support that part take on additional stress and strain, increasing the risk of injury in those areas and leading to the development of arthritis.

Stretching Exercises for the Upper Back and Shoulders

1. **Shoulder Shrug.** In any position (lying down, sitting, or standing), slowly raise up your shoulders. Hold them in that position for a few seconds and slowly lower them as far as you can, again holding them there for a few seconds. Return your shoulders to the normal position and repeat five times.

2. **Pillowcase Arm Circles.** Place a can of soup or other object of similar weight in a pillowcase. Hold the pillowcase in your hand and let your arm dangle at your side. Slowly rotate your arm in a circle, first clockwise ten times and then counterclockwise ten times. Repeat with the other arm.

3. **Walking the Wall.** Stand facing a wall at arm's length. With your elbows and wrists straight, slowly walk your fingers up the wall with your arms straight at the wrist and the elbow. Go as high as you can without causing pain. Repeat ten times. Turn to the right and repeat the exercise ten times with your left arm, then turn to the left and do it with your right arm. You can make a mark on the wall with a pencil to see how high you are able to raise your shoulder, then try to increase by one finger width how high you are able to go each day.

4. **Sitting Shoulder Flexion.** Sit in a chair with your back straight and your buttocks against the back of the chair, arms hanging at your sides. Place your palms and forearms together in front of

you, elbows bent. Lift your arms upward and reach above your head. Straighten your arms over your head and gradually lower them down to the side. Repeat five times. This exercise can also be done while lying on the floor on your back.

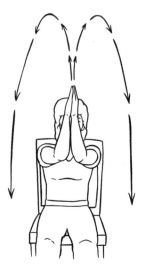

5. **Sitting Arm Butterfly.** Sit on a chair and lock your hands behind your head, elbows bent. Slowly move your elbows forward and then backward as far as you can. Keep your shoulders down as you move. Repeat five times.

6. **Windmills.** Extend your arms out to the sides of your body. Slowly start making small circles with your arms, keeping your elbows and wrists straight, making larger and larger circles as you go. Repeat in the opposite direction.

7. **Arm Crossover.** Stand with your arms at your sides, elbows straight. Cross your arms in front of you. Lower your arms back to your side, then extend them behind you, trying to cross them at the wrist behind your back. Repeat five times. You should feel a stretch in the upper back.

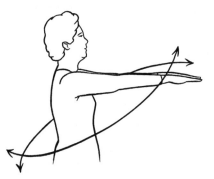

8. **Single Shoulder Grab.** Stand with arms hanging at your sides. Reach your right arm across the front of your body and hold your shoulder. Gently twist toward the right and hold for three seconds. Repeat five times, then do the motion five times on the other side. This exercise can be done either sitting or standing, although standing is preferable.

9. **Double Shoulder Grab.** Cross your arms over your chest and hold your right shoulder with your left hand and your left shoul-

der with your right hand. Gently twist to the right, slightly pulling your left shoulder forward. Repeat in the other direction. Complete the cycle five times. This can be done either sitting or standing, although standing is preferable.

10. **Elbow Grab.** Standing up, extend your right arm straight out in front of you. With your left hand, grab your right arm just above the elbow. Pull the right arm across your body at chest level and hold for three seconds. Relax, then do the same with the left arm. Repeat five times.

11. **Catching the Rain.** Stand up straight with your arms hanging at your sides. Extend your right arm out to your side parallel with the ground with your palm up. Lean gradually to the left. Return to the neutral position. Repeat five times on both sides.

Elbows

The elbows are less commonly affected by osteoarthritis than many of the other joints of the body. Usually people who have osteoarthritis of the elbow have had some sort of previous trauma to the joint, such as a fracture or dislocation. However, because of the importance of the elbow in all functions of the arm, maintaining strength and flexibility in this joint is essential, especially if you play such sports as tennis, golf, or baseball. Although some of the exercises intended for other joints will help the elbow as well, here are a couple of specific stretches you can do to keep your elbow joint loose.

Stretching Exercises for the Elbows

1. **Puppet Elbow Circles.** Stand straight and extend your arms out to your sides from your shoulders. Bend both arms at the elbow at a ninety-degree angle and let the lower half dangle as if you were a puppet. Make circles with your hands, keeping your wrists straight. Repeat ten times in both directions.

2. **Hand Flip.** Lying in bed or sitting in a chair with your arm straight out in front of you, turn your hand over while keeping your wrist firm. Repeat ten times on each side.

3. **Shoulder Touch.** Still lying in bed or sitting in a chair with your arms straight down at your sides, slowly bend your right arm at the elbow until your hand touches the front of your right shoulder. Lower it back down until it is straight again. Repeat ten times on each side.

Wrists, Hands, and Fingers

Stretching exercises for the wrists, hands, and fingers are sometimes the most difficult to visualize. You can clearly see how you can loosen up your back or your neck, but your fingers? Yet the small joints of the fingers and hands are among the most likely to develop arthritis. This is especially true for those of you who use your hands on a regular basis, such as laborers, carpenters, secretaries, or anyone who uses the computer on a regular basis. Mobility of the fingers and prevention of injury is as crucial for these as for any other parts of the body. I am sure all of you know someone who over time has developed nodules on the hands and at the base of the thumb, making it difficult and painful to open a jar or type. Simple stretches of the fingers can help you to prevent damage and relieve stiffness associated with arthritis.

Some wonder whether cracking your knuckles can lead to the development of arthritis. The answer is no. Although few studies (if any) look at this subject, not a single piece of evidence exists to support this old wives' tale. The sound you hear when you crack your knuckles is gas being released from the joint, not damage to the cartilage. This is not to say that forceful cracking cannot lead to damage of the joint, but gentle cracking has never been associated with the long-term development of arthritis.

Although knuckle cracking may not be the preferred method of stretching the joints of the hand, here are a few others you might find helpful.

Stretching Exercises for the Wrists, Hands, and Fingers

1. **Wrist Circles.** Hold your right wrist loosely with your left hand. Gently rotate your right wrist in all four directions. Repeat ten times with each hand.

2. **Wrist Glide.** Place your hand on a flat surface, such as a table or a desk, and move your wrist from side to side as far as you can. Repeat ten times with each wrist.

3. **Fist Circles.** Make a fist. Keeping it closed, rotate your wrist in a circle both clockwise and counterclockwise. Do ten times with each hand.

4. **Finger Splays.** Make a fist with both hands. Open your fingers gently and splay them apart as wide as you can. Make a fist again. Repeat ten times. Then make a fist and straighten your hand out, this time keeping your fingers pressed together. Repeat ten times.

5. **Thumb Touch.** With both hands, touch the tip of your thumb to the tip of your pinky on the same hand. Touch the tip of each finger in succession and wait for one second before going on to the next finger. Repeat ten times.

6. **Thumb Grab.** With both hands, extend your thumbs across your palms. Close your fist around your thumb and hold gently. Move your wrist from side to side and then in a circular motion both clockwise and counterclockwise ten times.

7. **Prayer Push.** Place your palms together. Gently and slowly push your palms away from each other with your fingers, without overstretching or cracking your knuckles. Repeat ten times.

8. **Finger Stretch.** Place your fingers together with your hands straight out. Gently spread your fingers apart and back together ten times.

Muscle Strength and Endurance

You have begun a regular joint flexibility program and you are starting to feel better, but you still have significant pain. Your joints are moving more freely, but walking, exercising, and bending still cause some pain. Now you are ready to start the second phase of the exercise program—muscle strengthening.

Lower Back

Back injuries are among the most common causes of disability in the United States. Back pain can prevent you from working, exercising, sleeping well, or playing with your children and grandchildren. Earlier in this section, we learned that it's important to "loosen up" your back and to use an appropriate lifting technique in order to prevent back injury. Keeping your back muscles strong and healthy can go a long way toward preventing future disability.

As with the knee, other muscle groups may be just as important in preventing the ravages of back pain and arthritis—most notably, the abdominal muscles. Increasing strength and flexibility in your abdominal muscles can take a great load off your back and reduce pain, or help to lower the risk of injury. Many people assume that situps are the best exercise to increase abdominal strength, but you may find that your back pain increases when doing them, especially if you already have arthritis or disk disease. The exercises listed here will help you to increase strength in your back and abdomen.

Strength Exercises for the Lower Back

1. **Partial Situp.** Lie on your back with your knees bent. Slowly raise your head and neck up off the ground while tightening your abdominal muscles. Breathe out (exhale) while you are doing this. You do not need to lift your back off the ground, and initially you should avoid doing so. Hold for one to two seconds and return to the floor, relaxing your abdominal muscles and taking in a deep breath (inhale). Start with five to ten of these modified situps and increase by one to two per week.

2. **Leg Lift.** Lie flat on your back with your legs straight out. Try to lift your legs about four to six inches off the ground. If you can, hold them for up to five seconds while exhaling. You should feel your abdominal muscles tightening. Slowly lower your legs back to the ground. Repeat up to five times. As you get stronger, after raising your legs off the ground you can try to slowly spread them apart and bring them back together after you have held them up for five seconds. This exercise may be very tough at first—if you can do it only once and hold it for only a second,

that's OK. Try to increase by one repetition or one second each week.

3. **Bicycle Kick.** While lying on your back with your knees bent, lift your legs off the ground and move your legs as though you are riding a bicycle. Do this for fifteen to thirty seconds.

4. **Reverse Situp.** Sit down on a sturdy stool (without a back). Place your feet flat on the floor and slowly lean back, up to six inches, keeping your back straight. Hold for up to five seconds, then slowly sit back up. Repeat five to ten times.

5. **Lying Quadriceps Strengthener.** Lie on your back with both knees bent. Slowly straighten one of your legs and lift your foot off the ground. Hold for up to five seconds, then bring the leg back down. You should feel a tightening of the muscles in your

lower back and buttocks. Repeat five times, then repeat five times with the other leg.

6. **Lying Quadriceps Strengthener with Arm Extension.** Do the lying quadriceps strengthener, but straighten your opposite arm and put it over your head while you are straightening your leg. This makes the exercise slightly more challenging. Repeat five times on both sides.

7. **Back Arch.** Lie on your stomach with your arms and legs stretched out. Lift your arms and legs off the ground simultaneously while arching your back. Hold for a couple of seconds, then relax. Repeat five times.

8. **Hip and Arm Extension.** Get down on your hands and knees and keep your back straight and your head up. Straighten out one leg and the opposite arm while keeping your abdominal muscles tight. Bring them back down and repeat with the other leg and arm. Complete five repetitions.

The exercises listed here should get you headed in the right direction. Although more exercises exist for the back and abdomen, most people can complete these in about five minutes, allowing you to strengthen your back without disrupting your daily routine.

Knees

As you know by now, increasing the range of motion of the joints will improve function and decrease stiffness. Strengthening the muscles and other structures around the joints will further diminish pain and improve function. The best example of this is in the quadriceps muscles in the thigh. Study after study has shown that increasing the strength of your quadriceps can reduce the pain from osteoarthritis of the knee. Even if you do not have arthritis of the knee, if you have strong quadriceps you are significantly less likely to suffer from pain and stiffness related to osteoarthritis.

Heather is a twenty-one-year-old amateur skier. Every winter she goes to Colorado to spend two to four weeks on the slopes, and she sneaks away for ski weekends as often as she can. She has seen several of her friends injure their knees while taking a spill on the slopes and is determined not to let that happen to her. Every day during the ski season and three days a week during the off-season, she does an aggressive quadriceps-strengthening program, along with other strengthening exercises. When she skis, she always stretches prior to getting on the slopes. So far, she has managed to avoid significant injury.

Jack is a sixty-five-year-old salesman who tore cartilage in his right knee about fifteen years ago when he tripped walking down a flight of stairs. He had arthroscopy to repair the tear, but over the past year began noticing increasing pain and stiffness in the knee. He had to give up golfing because of the pain. The knee would swell up on occasion and he was no longer able to walk long distances. Based on his history, exam, and an x-ray, Jack's family doctor diagnosed him with early arthritis a couple of months ago. He began a series of quadriceps-strengthening exercises, which have reduced the pain significantly. He is walking with greater ease and almost no discomfort and is ready to return to the golf course.

Some of the exercises for the quadriceps and other muscles around the knee can be done using a Swiss ball. A Swiss ball is a large round lightweight ball that can enhance the effectiveness of certain exercises. They are very inexpensive (usually less than twenty dollars).

Strength Exercises for the Knees

1. **Forward Lunge.** Stand up straight with your arms at your sides. Step forward with your left leg, bend both knees, and lower your trunk (center of your body) down. Stand back up slowly and repeat on the other side, stepping forward with your right leg. Do this five to ten times, trying to extend your leg slightly farther in front of you each week. Never bend your front knee beyond your front toe; your shin should be at a ninety-degree angle to the floor.

2. **Wall Squat.** Stand with your head, back, and buttocks placed firmly against a wall and your feet about eighteen inches from the wall. Begin with your legs straight. Contract your abdominal muscles. Slowly bend your legs and lower yourself until your thighs are parallel with the floor. Do not lock your knees. Slowly push back up. Repeat five to ten times. This exercise may be difficult at first. If you cannot lower yourself, just bend your knees slightly and maintain the position for five to ten seconds. As you advance with this exercise, you can make it even more challeng-

ing by placing a Swiss ball behind the small of your back as you do the motion. This forces you to use your leg and back muscles even more to maintain balance and position.

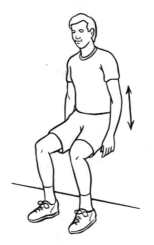

3. **Side Squat.** Stand with your left side next to a wall or table with your feet spread apart slightly and your right knee out in front a few inches. Holding on to the wall or table with your left hand, slowly bend your knees and lower yourself until your thighs are parallel with the floor. Keep your back straight and raise yourself back up. Again, as you bend your knee, don't let it go past your toes; your shin should form a ninety-degree angle with the floor.

4. **Lying Quadriceps Strengthener.** (See illustration on page 43.) Lie on your back with your knees bent and your feet flat on the floor. Slowly straighten your right leg at about a forty-five-degree angle to the floor while holding your abdominal muscles tight. Slowly return the leg to the bent position with your foot on the floor. Repeat with the left leg. Repeat five times initially, increasing by one repetition per week.

5. **Lying Thrust Kick.** Lie on your back with your knees bent and your feet flat on the floor. Lift both of your feet off the floor and

straighten your right leg. Hold for three seconds, then return the right leg to its starting position. Repeat with the left leg and do as many times as possible, although only three to five repetitions may be possible at first. This exercise and the lying quadriceps strengtheners will strengthen your abdominal muscles as well.

6. **Leg Curl.** Get down on your hands and knees. Tighten your abdominal muscles and straighten one leg out behind you. Keep your hips parallel with the floor and do not let your back sag. Return to the kneeling position slowly and repeat with the other leg. Do as many times as possible, though you may be able to do only a few repetitions of this at first.

7. **Leg Curl with Arm Extension.** (See illustration on page 44.) Get down on your hands and knees. Tighten your abdominal muscles and straighten one leg out behind you while straightening the opposite arm out in front of you, again keeping your hips parallel with the floor and not letting your back sag. Return the arm and leg to the rest position and repeat on the other side. Do as many times as possible. Do not try this until you can do the previous exercise (leg curl) with some confidence.

8. **Swiss Ball Side to Side.** Place a Swiss ball underneath the small of your back. Place your feet flat on the floor and keep your legs below the knee straight. Your knees should be flexed at a ninety-degree angle so that your thighs are parallel with the floor. With your legs, slowly move your whole body from one side to the

other, trying not to fall off the ball, but going as far as you can. Move from side to side and repeat five to ten times. This exercise helps build up not only your quadriceps, but your buttocks muscles as well. Make sure to do this exercise on a soft surface, such as a carpet, in case you fall. *Do not try this exercise if you have osteoporosis.*

As you progress with these exercises, you can add small one- to two-pound weights, especially on the leg lifts. In addition, if you want to make some of the stretching exercises more forceful and effective, you can add a device called a *Thera-Band*, an elastic band that increases resistance when you try to stretch it, like an oversized rubber band. You can get different levels of tension on Thera-Bands as your strength increases. Use them in any exercise where you would use your hand or a towel to pull your knee or any other part against resistance to increase muscle strength and flexibility. Unless you are in extremely poor shape, you can use a Thera-Band almost from the beginning. They're very inexpensive.

Quadriceps strengthening is essential not only for those who already have osteoarthritis of the knee, but for anyone who participates in an activity that can put significant strain on the knee joint. If you ski, jog, or play racquetball, basketball, soccer, or tennis, even on a casual basis, you may be able to prevent injury by doing quadriceps-strengthening exercises. Proper body mechanics and technique and appropriate equipment are obviously necessary as well, but you can improve your chances by keeping your quadriceps strong. Remember, preventing injury is the best way to prevent development of arthritis.

If you already have osteoarthritis, the good news is that exercises like these have been shown to significantly reduce arthritis pain and stiffness in a relatively short period of time. Some of the exercises may be difficult at first. If that is the case, try the ones that seem to be easiest for you and progress gradually. A visit to the physical therapist may give you guidance if you are severely limited. Trying some of these exercises in the pool may prove easier and take some of the strain off your joints.

Hips

Many of the muscles essential to keeping your knees in good shape also benefit the hips. In the same way, weakness or pain in your knee will put additional stress and strain on the hip and can lead to arthritic problems there. Strengthening the muscles and ligaments around the hip joint can provide you with substantial relief from the pain of arthritis if you already have it or help you to prevent it in the future, especially if you participate in activities that put stress and strain on that joint, such as rowing, martial arts, and high-impact aerobics.

> John is a thirty-two-year-old businessman who started taking martial arts classes about nine months ago. He began doing it once a week, but has now increased to three times a week. When he did his kicks, he noticed some discomfort in his buttocks muscles. He began a regimen of simple stretches and strength exercises of the hips and knees. Over several weeks he noticed not only a resolution of his pain, but greater ease in doing kicks.

Many of the exercises recommended for strengthening the knee will also strengthen the hip, but here are a few for you to try to improve muscle tone around the hip joint.

Strength Exercises for the Hips

1. **Buttocks Tightening.** While sitting in a chair, lying down, or standing, tighten the muscles of your buttocks and squeeze them together. Hold for five seconds and relax. Repeat five to ten times.

2. **Side (Hip Abductor) Kick.** With your left arm straight out to your side and against the wall for support, raise your right leg to the side as high as you can and try to hold it in the air for one to two seconds. Do this to the front and to the side. Repeat five times. Turn around and repeat the exercise with the opposite leg. This exercise may be difficult at first and can also be done in the

water if you have access to a warm water pool (see page 65 for more on warm water exercises).

3. **Sitting Leg Lift.** While sitting in a chair with a firm back, lift your legs off the ground until they are parallel with the floor. Slowly spread your legs apart and then bring them back together. Repeat five times.

4. **Waddle and Pigeon-Toed Walk.** Walk across a room in one direction with your feet turned outward, then walk back with your feet turned inward. Be careful not to lose your balance or twist your knee. Try to keep your knees pointing in the same direction as your toes.

5. **Lying (Hip Abductor) Kick.** Lie on your right side on the floor. Bend your right knee and straighten your left leg. Slowly lift the left leg off the ground as high as you can, then slowly lower it down. Repeat five times. Turn over and repeat the exercise on the other side.

Ankles and Feet

It may be more difficult for you to envision how to increase the "muscle tone" of your ankles and feet. Although you may realize that there must be muscles, tendons, and ligaments in the feet, it may be hard for you to imagine how increasing muscle strength in these areas will reduce or prevent joint pain. The principle is exactly the same as in the knee, but on a smaller scale. The stronger the small intrinsic muscles of the feet are, the more force they are able to absorb and the less stress and strain on the joints of your feet. This prevents damage to these joints, or diminishes the effect of any damage that already has occurred. The same principle applies to the hands as well.

Strength Exercises for the Ankles and Feet

1. **Tiptoe and Heel Walk.** Walk on your tiptoes across a room, then walk back on your heels. Repeat five times.

2. **Tiptoe and Heel Stand.** Stand facing a wall and extend your arms out so that your hands are flat against the wall. Your feet should be about a foot away from the wall. Begin with your feet flat on the ground. Slowly rise up onto your tiptoes and lower back to the ground. Then lift the front of your feet up and stand on your heels. Repeat five times.

3. **Toe Curl.** While sitting in a chair with a sturdy back and your feet flat on the ground, curl your toes as hard as you can into the floor. Hold for five seconds. Straighten your toes out and then, keeping them straight, push your toes down against the floor. Hold for five seconds. Repeat this cycle five times.

4. **Tissue Pickup.** Place a piece of tissue or toilet paper on the ground and pick it up with your toes. Repeat ten times with each foot. This will not only increase strength, but also improve coordination.

Neck, Upper Back, and Shoulders

Joints and muscles do not move in isolation. When you move your neck from one side to the other, over forty muscles and joints are involved. Although this section of the book separates exercises into different joint groups, significant overlap often exists. Certain exercises that stretch or strengthen muscle groups around one joint may benefit other joints as well. In this case, the neck, upper back, and shoulder are grouped together because there is so much overlap that separating them did not make any sense. Some would argue that strengthening the muscle around the shoulder girdle can be isolated in some cases from the others, and these exercises will be pointed out.

Casandra is a thirty-seven-year-old ad executive who spends much of her time chained to her desk. She does a lot of work at the computer during the week, but on weekends likes to go out biking and playing softball. She pitches and plays outfield. She began noticing pain in the back of her shoulders and neck after a long game. She also noticed her neck getting stiff at the end of the day. She would do some gentle stretches, which seemed to relieve most of the symptoms.

She went to see her doctor, who noted some tightness over the muscles of the back and shoulders, especially when she tried to lift her arms above her head or behind her back. She was advised to go to a physical therapist to learn some exercises, but her HMO refused to pay for it. She began a program of gentle stretches for the neck, upper back, and shoulders, initially ten to fifteen minutes a day. Her range of motion began to improve, but her muscles still felt tired at the end of the day or after she pitched six or seven innings.

Casandra started a strengthening program, and over the next several weeks began to see a change. She no longer felt fatigued at the end of a game or at the end of her workday. When she was in the outfield, she could now reach home plate on her throws, where before she had to bounce it in. She continues her fifteen-minute daily regimen to this day.

Strength Exercises for the Neck, Upper Back, and Shoulders

1. **Head-Hand Push.** Place your open hand against the side of your head. Push your head into your hand as hard as you can without moving it. Move your hand to the front of your head and the other side and perform the same exercise. Repeat five times.

2. **Head–Thera-Band Push.** With a Thera-Band or towel, place one end around your wrist and the other around your forehead. Apply gentle resistance with your neck in the opposite direction. Hold for five seconds and release slowly. Do this exercise forward and backward, to the right and to the left, but be careful not to do it too forcefully, as you can hurt yourself. Repeat five times in each direction.

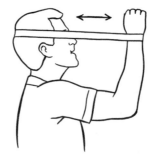

3. **Head-Wall Push.** Standing or sitting, place your head against a wall. Using your neck muscles, push against the wall. Do this with your forehead, sides of head, and back of head.

4. **Shoulder Extension and Flexion.** Take a one- to two-pound can of food in each hand (or use light handweights, if you have

them). Stand with your arms straight down at your sides. Keeping your arms straight, slowly raise your arms to the sides. Hold them parallel to the floor for two to three seconds and slowly lower them back to your sides. Repeat five times and do the same exercise with your arms moving straight out in front of you. You can increase the number of repetitions or the weight to increase the difficulty of this exercise as time goes on.

5. **Standing Sideways Pushup.** Stand next to a wall with your arm straight at your side. Place your hand and forearm against the wall and push against the wall. Hold for three to five seconds, then relax. Do this with both the back and the front of the hand and repeat five times. Switch to the other arm and perform the same exercise.

6. **Standing Forward Pushup.** Stand facing a wall with your head touching the wall and your elbows bent and your hands flat on the wall. Push your body and head away from the wall like you are doing a standing pushup. Lower yourself back to the wall and repeat ten times. Regular pushups are also good, but they are often too difficult. If you find that you would like to try regu-

lar pushups on the ground, start with the modified type: kneeling, keeping your knees bent and your trunk straight.

Once you have mastered these exercises, you can slowly add weights, using common household items to increase the difficulty. If you really want to push it, you can go to the local YMCA or other community facility and use the gym, but make sure you consult the staff and use the equipment appropriately, or you can really hurt yourself.

Elbows

Strengthening exercises for the elbows and arms are often the easiest for people to envision. You can all remember the bodybuilder with the big muscular arms doing curls and flexing to show off the size of his biceps. The muscles of the upper arms help to stabilize both the elbow and shoulder joints. You do not need to look like Mr. or Ms. Universe to have strong and healthy arms and protect these joints. Although the elbow is less prone to osteoarthritis than many other joints, strengthening muscles of the arm and forearm will also help you to protect your shoulders and wrists.

Strength Exercises for the Elbows

1. **Elbow Flexion.** Take a one-pound can in each hand. Begin with your arms at your sides. Slowly bend your arms at the elbow as far as you can, then slowly lower them down again. Repeat five

to ten times. You can do this without the cans initially, or use something heavier as you get stronger.

2. **Overhead Elbow Extension.** Stand with a wall at arm's length behind you. Take a one-pound can in each hand. Raise your arms straight over your head, keeping your shoulders down. Bend your arms at the elbow toward the wall behind you, and bring your hands as close to your shoulders as you can. Straighten your arms up slowly until they are back in their original position. Repeat five times. You can do this without a can initially if it is too difficult, or increase the number of repetitions or the weight as you get stronger.

3. **Desk Lift.** Put your forearms under a desk or table while sitting in a chair. Press up against the desk as though you were trying to lift it up. Be careful to put the pressure on your forearms and avoid straining your back, neck, or shoulders. Hold for three to five seconds, then relax. Repeat five times.

Wrists, Hands, and Fingers

We don't often think about strength in our wrists, hands, and fingers until something happens: we drop an expensive vase, can't open a can or jar, or lose control of the tennis racket. Simple activities such as writing, typing, cutting your food, or turning the ignition on the car can become more difficult when your hands become weak. There are many simple things you can do to increase the strength in your hands and wrists, and many of the exercises can be done while you are watching TV.

Strength Exercises for the Wrists, Hands, and Fingers

1. **Wrist Flexion and Extension.** Take a one-pound can in each hand. With your forearm resting on a table, bend your wrist up and down slowly and side to side. Perform this exercise five to ten times.

2. **Palm Press.** Place your palms against each other. Push them together as hard as you can without moving them. Hold for five seconds and repeat five times.

3. **Rubber Ball Squeeze.** Take a small rubber ball and squeeze it as tightly as you can. Repeat ten to fifteen times.

4. **Thumb Press.** Place the tip of your thumb against the tip of your next finger. Push them together as hard as you can. Hold for five seconds. Do the same with your thumb against each of your other fingers. Repeat five times.

5. **Tight Fist.** Close your fingers together as tight as you can. Hold for five seconds and relax. Repeat five times.

6. **Index Press.** Place the index finger of one hand against the sides of one of your fingers on the other hand. Push that finger against

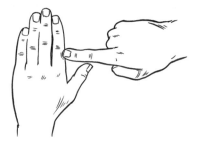

your index finger and hold for three seconds. Perform this exercise with all of your fingers on both hands and in both directions.

Strengthening exercises can always be made easier or more challenging. The goal is not for you to become a bodybuilder, but to strengthen the muscles and tendons around your joints so that you can prevent or retard damage. You should not be embarrassed if you cannot do as many repetitions as recommended or are unable to use the one-pound cans as described. Any increase in strength and flexibility can significantly improve your joints' capacity to absorb forces and therefore prevent injury. Small changes can result in significant increases in your ability to walk, jog, play tennis, or even in dressing and washing yourself if your arthritis is advanced. Regardless of your level of fitness, you can definitely enhance your activity level and your overall health.

Aerobic Exercise

Most of us think of *aerobic exercise* as those classes in the gym where people in leotards jump around to some hip-hop or disco music. Aerobic exercise is actually exercise that allows for general fitness of the muscles, joints, and heart. Any exercise that increases your heart rate for a sustained period can be considered an aerobic exercise. This includes aerobic classes, but also walking, swimming, biking, hiking, and other forms of more vigorous activity.

Studies have shown that people with osteoarthritis who do gentle aerobic exercise have significantly less joint pain and stiffness than people who do not exercise. Although there is little

Benefits of Aerobic Exercise

Improves joint motion and flexibility
Increases joint lubrication
Increases muscle tone and range of motion
Promotes weight loss
Prevents heart attack and stroke long term

doubt that joint-specific exercise is critical to reducing the pain and stiffness of arthritis, even a gentle aerobic exercise program such as walking can significantly reduce your pain. Not only that, but you feel better about yourself because you are out and doing something, rather than sitting around your house on your couch watching the latest stunts on afternoon talk shows.

You do not need to make a major commitment to see the benefits of aerobic exercise. If you are able to devote twenty to thirty minutes to it three times a week, you can begin to see the benefits. The amount of exercise you do may depend on your symptoms and your time constraints. Overdoing it, often a problem among athletes, such as football players and marathon runners, is not the best thing for your joints. If you do too much, the additional wear and tear on your joints can increase your risk of developing arthritis later in life. Recent studies, however, indicate that regular exercise, if done appropriately, does not lead to the development of arthritis. Previously it was thought that a lifetime of exercise exposed joints to more trauma and therefore damaged the cartilage, eventually leading to arthritis. In fact, studies have now demonstrated that this is far from true. People who do regular aerobic exercise certainly do not develop more arthritis, and probably suffer less from the pain of arthritis. Evidence is also clear that regular aerobic exercise can reduce symptoms in those who have osteoarthritis.

Many of my patients find aerobic exercise to be the easiest to start, as they can often find an activity they enjoy. Walking is probably the most common aerobic exercise adopted. Very few people are not capable of walking to some degree or another. If your arthritis is so severe that you cannot even walk, walking in a warm water pool may allow you to begin doing aerobic exercise with minimal stress and strain on your joints. There are other exercises that you can do in the water as well, and you do not need to know how to swim to do them. These exercises will be discussed later in this chapter.

Obviously, many of you are able to walk much more than half a block. Even if you do not have arthritis but are not physically active, finding an activity that you enjoy is essential for your long-term health. Pick something you like and don't overdo it. Often, when you have been inactive for a while your muscles and joints get weak and lose flexibility. If you try to do too much too soon, you are at risk for injury. So if you're planning on picking up rollerblading this weekend, be careful and make sure to loosen up and do some of the stretching exercises described earlier in this chapter.

Walking

Walking is probably the easiest and one of the best types of aerobic exercise. You don't need any equipment except for comfortable walking shoes, and it can be done almost anywhere. You can walk indoors when the weather is inclement, and many shopping malls around the country have set up walking "trails" that allow you to judge how well you are doing (of course they hope that you will stop and shop, but you are certainly not required to do so). Some people prefer to walk outdoors, while some like to use a treadmill. The most important thing is finding a place and possibly a person you like to walk with and getting started.

The biggest complaint people have about walking is that it is "boring." There are many tricks you can do to maintain your interest and push you to keep going.

1. Get a buddy to walk with. When one of you doesn't feel like going, the other will push that one to go. Also, the social interaction helps to pass the time, and often you will push each other to go farther or faster.

2. Take a path that you like, and alter it if you start to get bored. For instance, some people like to walk through a busy shopping area and people-watch, while others prefer to walk on a forest trail. Just make sure that the ground is not too uneven, as you could twist your ankle or knee. If you begin to grow bored or disenchanted with your route, change it.

3. Do something while you are walking. If you walk alone, listen to music during your walk or bring your dog. If you use the treadmill, set it up so you can watch your favorite program or read a book or newspaper throughout your walk.

4. Wear comfortable clothes in layers. Once you start walking, you may start to build up a sweat, even on a cold day. Take a sweater or jacket you can easily tie around your waist.

You can start your walking program based on your fitness level. An easy rule to start with is twenty minutes a day, three to four times per week. You may be able to walk only a half-mile or up to three miles during the twenty minutes, depending on how good of shape you are in to begin with. If you can walk for a longer period of time or more days a week, even better. Every week or so, try to increase the distance you walk, even if it is only by one or two driveways or by a minute or two. As time goes on, you will find that you are able to walk faster and farther. Pushing yourself to do more is another way to maintain interest in the exercise that you are doing, whether it's walking or anything else. Not only will this improve your aerobic capacity, but it helps to stretch and strengthen your lower back, hips, knees, ankles, and feet. Numerous studies have shown that a regular walking program can significantly reduce the pain of osteoarthritis.

If you are severely disabled from the pain of your arthritis, you may be able to walk only short distances, even just to the end of your driveway, or for only two to three minutes. That's OK. A little exercise is better than none. If you are significantly limited by your symptoms, start very gradually. If you can only get to the neighbor's house and back, that's fine. Start doing that on a daily basis. After about one to two weeks, see if you can get to the neighbor's house two houses away, or at least part of the way there. Try to increase by a small amount every one to two weeks if possible. You might be surprised to find within a couple of months that you're able to make it to the end of the block and back and that your pain isn't quite as severe as before. If pain is limiting you from accomplishing even that much, you may need to consider medication (discussed in "The Third Quarter" and "The Fourth Quarter").

Bicycling

So, you watched the Tour de France and have decided that you want to be like Lance Armstrong and ride hundreds of miles a day. Although bicycling is a wonderful way to increase muscle strength, flexibility, and fitness, it is not for everyone. Many people with osteoarthritis find that it's hard on the knees and can actually lead to increased pain. Some of this may result from having the seat at an improper height, leading to increased stress on your knee joints. However, even if the bike is adjusted properly, you may still have knee pain. If this is the case, bicycling is probably not for you. In addition, if you have lower-back pain, you may find that bicycling increases pain and stiffness in your back. Recumbent bicycles (stationary bicycles with back support that you ride while sitting down) may be an option for you.

If you choose to start cycling, either outdoors or indoors (with a stationary bicycle), start slowly. Many people feel great when they first get on the bike and start riding and riding and riding, then suddenly find themselves eight miles from home with aching legs and wondering how they will get back home. When you start, stay in your neighborhood and don't wander too far. When your legs begin to hurt, head for home. You may be able to go only a mile or two initially, and only at five to ten miles per hour. You should try to start at fifteen to twenty minutes per day, three times per week, and gradually increase over time.

Many of the techniques suggested for keeping you interested in walking also apply to cycling. If you decide to outdoor cycle, it is imperative that you have not only an appropriate bicycle that is set at the correct height, but that you wear all of the necessary protective equipment, such as a helmet and elbowpads and kneepads. And if you are going to ride at night, use all of the necessary reflectors and wear highly visible clothing.

Yoga and Tai Chi

Yoga and tai chi have been around for thousands of years, but have been recently rediscovered in American culture. Yoga allows you to put your joints through a wide range of motions while incorporating appropriate breathing and relaxation techniques. Beginning yoga is very gentle, and you can participate in it even if you are severely limited by arthritis. As your mobility improves, yoga can become more challenging, giving you not only a wonderful aerobic and stretching workout, but a very potent muscle strengthening exercise as well. Yoga is a difficult activity to learn on your own, but inexpensive classes are widely available. Just make sure your instructor is well trained so that you don't overdo it and get yourself hurt.

Tai chi is the most ancient of the martial arts, using gentle motions to improve balance and flexibility. If you have ever been to China, you probably saw thousands of people in parks every morning practicing tai chi. It is very safe and easy, but usually requires some form of instruction. It has been shown to potentially reduce your risk of falls and fractures if you suffer from osteoporosis, and is an excellent way to loosen up and make you feel steadier on your feet. Classes are available in many parts of the country as the popularity of tai chi grows.

Swimming

Swimming is one of the best forms of exercise. It is easier on your joints than most other activities and works many muscles and joints simultaneously. It also burns more calories than almost any other activity when done vigorously, so it can be an especially good choice if you are trying to lose weight. The water allows you to move your joints more freely and is an excellent alternative if walking and other activities are a problem.

Obviously, not everyone has access to a pool, and even some who do still cannot use it year-round because it is outside. Your local YMCA often has indoor pools and they are present in almost every community. For a nominal price, you can have access to a well-heated pool almost every day. Again, the rule of starting slowly and working your way up is important. If you can swim three times a week for twenty minutes, that's a good start. If you can do more, great; if you can go only five minutes, that's OK too. Every week, try to increase by one more lap, or by one or two minutes, time permitting. Your heart, muscles, and joints will thank you.

Other Aerobic Exercises

You might not enjoy individual exercises, such as walking, swimming, or biking, but you still need to get into shape. Although bowling may not count, many other sports can increase your fitness in a socially interactive context. Sports such as basketball, tennis, and soccer provide a great aerobic workout. If the gym is more your style, consider trying a low-impact aerobics or spinning class.

With any activity, it's important to not overdo it. Equally important is to properly warm up before starting the activity. In the final chapter, stretching and strengthening exercises for distinct athletic activities will be reviewed. If you haven't been active for a while, start nice and easy, because injury often comes when you are not physically capable of doing an activity, or when your body gets tired and does not compensate appropriately for a particular movement. Remember, the best way to prevent arthritis is to prevent the initial injury from occurring.

Sometimes, however, you are so out of shape or your arthritis is so severe that even a simple walking program is impossible. Don't give up hope. There is still a type of exercise that you can do to improve your level of fitness, decrease the pain and stiffness of your joints, and to regain a more active lifestyle: warm water exercises.

Warm Water Exercises

The pool is not only for those who can swim. Many people with moderate to severe arthritis are not able to do even the simplest exercise regimen without significant pain and discomfort. As your arthritis worsens, your joints lose mobility and become stiffer and more painful. Your muscles get weaker and less flexible, further compounding the problem. Warm water (usually eighty-six to ninety degrees) helps to relax stiff muscles and joints. This usually allows your joints to move more easily and improve your flexibility. The warm water essentially breaks the cycle of increasing pain and stiffness and allows you to begin exercising again.

Warm water exercise does not involve swimming, so you do not need to be a good swimmer to exercise in the water. Many of the exercises described earlier in this section can be performed in the water as well, although some exercises are unique to the pool. Water has natural resistance, which allows you to build muscle tone without some of the difficulties you may have with land-based therapy. In addition, the buoyancy of the water reduces the impact on your joints when you do certain activities. For example, many people who have problems walking on land are able to walk in the water. As you initiate a water exercise program, you begin to move and loosen up your joints. Muscle tone improves and you become more flexible. As flexibility improves, pain begins to diminish and you are able to do more, eventually even walk distances on land. As your activity in the pool increases, you naturally meet more resistance in the water, and the workout slowly becomes more challenging.

> Mary is a seventy-eight-year-old woman who was suffering from severe arthritis for many years. She had severe pain and stiffness in her neck, shoulders, back, hips, and knees. She tried numerous different medications with only moderate success, and continued to require a cane or walker to get around. She had to have friends do all of her shopping for her. She came to my office and I advised her to start a series of pool exercises at the local YMCA. She began with very gentle stretches and gradually progressed to walking. Over a three-month period she has noted significant improvement in her pain and flexibility and no longer requires the walker. Mary is now able to walk two to three blocks with a cane, do her own shopping, and go out to lunch with her friends—all activities she had not done for several years.

Here are a few water exercises to try.

1. **Water Jog.** Jog in the water for five minutes.

2. **Water Hip Abduction and Flexion.** Stand by the side of the pool and hold on with one hand. Stretch your opposite leg out to the side at the hip. Bring it back down to the bottom of the pool. Lift the same leg out in front of your body. Repeat this cycle five times, then turn around and repeat it five times with the other leg.

3. **Water Kick.** Holding on at the side of the pool, kick in the water for five minutes. As you advance, you can do the same with a kickboard.

4. **Water Windmills.** Standing in the water up to your neck, place your arms out at your sides. Begin making small circles with your arms, gradually getting bigger each time. You can increase strength and make the exercise more difficult by opening your hands in the water. This creates more resistance as you try to push against the water.

5. **Water Two-Legged Hop.** Standing with your legs straight, push off the bottom of the pool with your feet. Go up and down ten to fifteen times.

Almost all of the exercises in this chapter can easily be modified for the pool. If you are not sure what to do, the Arthritis Foundation offers "Twinges and Hinges" classes at pools all over the country.

Warm water exercises can be a wonderful jump-start to an arthritis exercise program. Swimming is an excellent aerobic exercise that also improves joint and muscle strength and mobility. It is a wonderful way to prevent the development of osteoarthritis while maintaining a high level of fitness. Swimming allows you to put your joints through a wide range of motion without some of the wear and tear caused by aggressive land-based exercises.

Swimming should not be confused with warm water exercises. You don't need to know how to swim to do warm water exercises. You don't even have to be able to float. If you can swim and have access to a pool, then start right away. Swimming is not only good for your joints, it is good for your heart as well. In fact, many specialists think that swimming is the "perfect" aerobic exercise. Swimming increases heart rate, improves muscle tone (including all of those important muscles we worked in the strengthening exercises in this chapter), and allows joints to work in unison in a free and active motion. Varying your swim stroke (from crawl to breaststroke, for example) can allow you to work different muscle groups.

If you haven't been in the pool for a while, start slowly. You may be able to do only one stroke for five to ten minutes. Gradually increase your time in the pool by one minute per week, or try to increase by one lap per week. Over time, you will have a nearly complete arthritis and cardiovascular workout. Although swimming is a wonderful exercise, it is important to continue to do your joint-specific exercises if you have problems with particular joints.

People who enjoy swimming will often use the excuse that they don't have access to a pool, or that the pool they have access to is too hot, too cold, too crowded, too dirty, or outside and the weather is never right. Most areas of the country have local well-maintained public pools that have generous hours and provide easy access for people wanting to initiate an exercise program. Call your local park district, chamber of commerce, or the Arthritis Foundation for a list of pools near you.

The Final Play

Setting up your own exercise program depends on what your goals are. If you are a casual athlete who wants to avoid injury and damage to your joints, your exercises may be very different from those of someone who already has advanced arthritis and is happy just to be able to walk in the supermarket. The most important lesson is to start with a plan and to stick to it. If you find exercises that you enjoy you will be much more likely to stick with them. Diagramming your own strategy is essential to winning the war over osteoarthritis.

You've now learned how you can do exercises that will help prevent injury and the development of arthritis in the future. But only you can start a program to win the war over the pain and stiffness of osteoarthritis. Exercise is your first key to preventing and treating this disabling disease.

Nutrition and Vitamins

"The First Quarter" spent a great deal of time reviewing the various types of exercise that can help you to prevent or reduce the symptoms of osteoarthritis. "The Second Quarter" is devoted to developing and maintaining a healthy diet, something *you* can do to prevent and reduce the symptoms of osteoarthritis. Maintaining an ideal body weight is crucial in overcoming the pain and stiffness of arthritis. If you are overweight, simply losing some of those excess pounds can markedly diminish your symptoms. But what if you are not overweight? Is there anything you can do to lower your risk of developing arthritis? Absolutely.

In "The Second Quarter" you will find:

- An explanation of the importance of *ideal body weight* in preventing arthritis and alleviating arthritis symptoms
- An exploration of foods and supplements that can help you overcome arthritis
- A review of the model arthritis diet

Ideal Body Weight and Arthritis

The importance of maintaining a healthy weight is well established today. The health benefits of staying thin have been touted for years and are certainly not limited to arthritis relief.

If you already have a weight problem and suffer from any of the conditions associated with an unhealthy weight, you can significantly reduce your symptoms simply by losing weight.

In the Introduction we learned how being overweight could lead to the development of arthritis. Extra body weight puts increased stress and strain on joints and the surrounding ligaments, tendons, and muscles. The heavier you are, the greater force is transmitted to the cartilage. This can lead to the development of microdamage, small tears in the cartilage. Slowly, the cartilage begins to wear away and the process of arthritis has begun. In addition, people who are overweight tend to have weaker muscles and ligaments relative to their body weight, placing them at even greater risk of injury and damage.

Getting your weight down to a healthy level, or even losing ten or twenty pounds, can have an enormous impact on your symptoms and help to prevent or reduce the pain and stiffness of arthritis.

Health Benefits of Maintaining an Ideal Body Weight

Prevents diabetes
Prevents high blood pressure
Prevents heart disease and
    stroke
Prevents peripheral vascular
    disease
Prevents varicose veins
Prevents osteoarthritis
Lowers cholesterol

Maria is a fifty-five-year-old ad executive who has been about thirty to fifty pounds overweight her entire life. She has a job that does not require any physical activity, and she gets very little exercise. She began noticing pain in her hips and knees about three years ago. The symptoms started with difficulty getting in and out of a chair at work. Eventually it became painful to walk up and down stairs or to do anything more strenuous than walking briskly. She would generally eat her largest meal late at night, around 8:30, and go to sleep about 10. She would often skip breakfast and "just grab something" for lunch. She frequently snacked on candy during the afternoon and before she went to bed.

Maria embarked on a plan of healthy eating and gentle exercise that involved eating a nutritious breakfast, packing a well-balanced lunch, and eating a lighter dinner around 7. She avoided eating between meals. She began losing weight almost immediately, an average of about a pound a week. Over the next few months, Maria began noticing that her hips and knees didn't hurt so much and that walking or getting out of a chair became a lot easier. As her activity level increased, she noticed that despite the fact that she had only minimally decreased her caloric intake, she was able to keep off the twenty-five pounds that she had lost. Her blood pressure, which had been up to 140, had decreased to 120, and her energy level improved markedly. She has now maintained this regimen for two years.

How do you determine what your ideal body weight is? There are a lot of fancy charts based on body frame and a number of other measures, but a simple formula that doctors use can help you to get a general idea of where you should be. For women, if you are 5 feet tall, your ideal weight is 100 pounds plus 5 pounds for every additional inch of height:

$$100 + (5 \times \text{the number of inches above 5 feet}) = \text{ideal body weight}$$

For example, if you are 5 feet 4 inches tall, your ideal weight is 120 pounds:

$$100 + (5 \times 4 \text{ inches}) = 120 \text{ pounds}$$

For men, because they have denser bones and higher muscle content, the formula is slightly different. If you are a man who is 5 feet tall, your ideal weight is 106 pounds, and you add 6 pounds for every additional inch:

$$106 + (6 \times \text{the number of inches above 5 feet}) = \text{ideal body weight}$$

So if you are 5 feet 9 inches tall, your ideal weight is 160 pounds:

$$106 + (6 \times 9 \text{ inches}) = 160 \text{ pounds}$$

You can add 10 percent if you have a large frame or subtract 10 percent if you have a small frame. If you are within about 5 percent of this number, you are doing OK. Obviously this does not take into account such factors as age, body frame, and so on, but it is a good estimate of where you should be. As you get older, specifically over the age of sixty, you can increase the upper end of the estimate by another 5 to 10 percent, as there is evidence for general health purposes that a slightly higher body weight may be beneficial as you get older.

These are estimates *only*, and what is ideal for one person may not be ideal for another. In addition, if you are already significantly overweight, a target of losing an enormous amount of weight may not only be unrealistic, but also discourage you from losing anything. For example, if you are a man hovering around 270 pounds and are 5 feet 11 inches, your "ideal weight" is 172 pounds. Try setting an initial goal that is much more realistic, such as losing 20 to 30 pounds. You can realize a great benefit for your joints and overall health with that amount of weight loss, even if you have not reached your ideal weight.

Always set realistic goals for yourself. Many people start a diet with the expectation of losing 50 pounds in two weeks, and when that doesn't happen they give up and return to their old bad habits. Diets abound, all promising to provide the secret of how to lose weight quickly and easily, without any ill effects. You have tried every one of them: high protein, low protein, high fat, low fat, liquid, cantaloupe, watermelon, and nutmeg. And although you have lost weight with each one, the weight never seems to stay off.

The reason is quite simple. You need to change the way you look at food so that you are able to maintain a lifestyle change. Quick solutions for rapid weight loss do not change the most fundamental problem: the need to establish a regular healthy eating pattern and stick to it. Most fad diets allow you to lose weight because you begin to make the effort to watch what you are eating. If you begin to watch your eating habits and caloric intake in any kind of regimented fashion, you almost certainly will lose weight. However, if the diet is not one you can maintain for your lifetime, then the weight will come right back as soon as you stop.

Are There Foods or Vitamins That May Help Prevent or Treat Arthritis?

Over the years, many foods and vitamins have been touted to prevent the development of osteoarthritis or reduce and reverse its progress and symptoms. Other foods have even been implicated as a cause of arthritis. Is there any truth to the idea that some foods or vitamins may actually help or hurt? There is a growing body of evidence that particular substances found in certain foods may serve as natural anti-inflammatories and help slow down the development of arthritis. A healthy, well-balanced diet is essential for healthy joints and muscles, but more specific recommendations may help to give you the extra edge in your battle against this disease.

Whole Foods Versus Refined Foods

There has been a great deal of debate in the nutritional literature as to the benefits of whole foods versus refined foods. Whole foods are those that are in their so-called "natural state," not having been "refined" or pasteurized. Most dairy and fruit juices sold in supermarkets are pasteurized, a process that eliminates harmful bacteria and other organisms that can cause serious infections. Flour and sugar are usually refined, and some of the vitamins and minerals contained in these products may be lost during the process. Some believe that by refining or pasteurizing a food, you may not only eliminate known beneficial nutrients, but unknown ones as well.

You do not necessarily have to run down to the local health food store to find "whole foods." Many of these are foods you think of every day, including raw fruits and vegetables (not frozen), as well as beans, nuts, unprocessed grains, and seeds. In other words, when you eat an orange or banana, a carrot or celery, or some sunflower seeds, you are eating whole foods. Unpasteurized juices, breads made with unrefined flour, and soybeans are considered whole foods as well. Obviously, not all whole foods are created equal, and some are healthier than others—for example, some nuts contain high levels of saturated fats. In addition, if not treated properly, unpasteurized dairy products and juices contain a risk of infection, although this has become much less common than it was in the 1800s when pasteurization was originally developed, as sanitation and screening techniques have improved.

People who eat whole foods tend to consume more fiber and nutrients, with fewer saturated fats and sugars, than people who do not eat many whole foods. It is also clear that people who eat more saturated fats and sugars are at higher risk for a number of diseases, including heart disease, diabetes, cancer, and possibly arthritis. Whether the benefits seen are specifically related to the whole foods and the nutrients they may provide is unclear, but the whole-food debate does illustrate the importance of a healthy, well-balanced diet full of fresh fruits and vegetables and grains high in fiber, all of which have been linked to improved health and well-being. Few argue against the notion that eating more oranges, grapes, bananas, broccoli, asparagus, and cauliflower, and fewer candy bars, danishes, and chocolate, is a bad thing. Most whole foods are safe and nutritious—why not give them a try?

Omega-3 Fatty Acids

Omega-3 fatty acids are natural anti-inflammatories. They are most commonly found in fish such as mackerel, tuna, and salmon. Studies have shown that when omega-3 fatty acids are given in high doses as a supplement, they can have an anti-inflammatory effect similar to that of prescription nonsteroidal anti-inflammatory drugs (see "The Third Quarter" for more details on these medications). Unfortunately, the patients taking these supplements also had a higher rate of bloating, gas, and diarrhea. These fatty acids counteract the body's inflammatory response by preventing the production of substances in the body called *prostaglandins* and *leukotrienes*, which contribute to the development of inflammation. Diets rich in omega-3 fatty acids have been shown to reduce risk of heart disease. The benefits of omega-3 fatty acids were originally discovered in Eskimos, who consume a much larger quantity of fish than most people and were found to have lower rates of heart disease.

Fatty acids are contained in many different foods, including fish and vegetables, and come in many shapes and sizes. *Alpha-linolenic acid* is an omega-3 fatty acid that is found predominantly in green vegetables and is found in high concentrations in flaxseed oil. *Eicosapentaenoic acid*, another of the omega-3s, is found in fish, such as salmon and sardines. *Gamma-linolenic acid*, an omega-6 fatty acid that can be found in evening primrose oil, may also have natural anti-inflammatory effects by producing "good" prostaglandins that do not promote inflammation. Some smaller studies have been done in other forms of arthritis with evening primrose oil to determine whether it provides any benefit, and the results have been mixed.

Although the benefits of omega-3 fatty acids have been shown in heart disease and rheumatoid arthritis, no formal studies have been done to determine its effects on osteoarthritis. Until recently, it was not recognized that osteoarthritis was an inflammatory disease, so using a natural anti-inflammatory to help treat this condition was not considered. The role of inflammation in osteoarthritis is now much better understood. Whether these fatty acids will help you is not entirely clear, but in light of its established benefits in other diseases, adding fish and vegetables to your diet that contain omega-3 fatty acids certainly seems like a good idea.

Nightshade Foods

Nightshade foods contain an alkaloid called *solanine*, which has been reported (in one book) to cause morning stiffness, lead to cartilage degeneration, and prevent the natural repair process of cartilage. Foods that contain solanine include tomatoes, potatoes, eggplant, peppers, and chiles. Although one informal study claimed that patients with arthritis who avoided these foods reported a significant decrease in arthritic symptoms, no well-done studies to date have supported this notion. You can avoid these items if you choose, but understand that doing so will not likely significantly improve your arthritis symptoms.

Bioflavonoids

Bioflavonoids are plant pigments that are responsible for the colors of plants and flowers. They help plants avoid damage from the environment and have been credited with a wide variety of biological effects, including functioning as natural antioxidants and anti-inflammatories, and even having anti-tumor effects. Bioflavonoids are found in numerous fruits, including berries, cherries, and citrus, as well as buckwheat, cabbage, and onions. They are contained in the skin and center of the fruit.

It has been claimed that bioflavonoids can protect you against the ravages of arthritis through a number of different mechanisms. These include:

1. Supporting your body's ability to manufacture cartilage and preventing cartilage from being destroyed during joint inflammation
2. Reducing the body's inflammatory response
3. Preventing cellular damage from free radicals and other oxidants by scavenging these by-products
4. Improving tissue healing after injury
5. Decreasing production of inflammatory mediators from white blood cells

Very few randomized studies (if any) have looked at the potential beneficial effects of bioflavonoids, although many of the foods listed with bioflavonoids can easily be included in a well-balanced and healthy diet. The lack of studies does not imply that these substances do not do what they are said to do, and incorporating them into your regular eating plan is not risky.

Antioxidants

Antioxidants have been hailed for years as the miracle to slow down the aging process, including slowing down or preventing the progression of arthritis. It is thought that cellular damage is the result of *free radicals*, molecules that supposedly attack and destroy healthy tissue. Activity of these molecules is increased in states of inflammation. Antioxidants work by binding with these free radicals and preventing them from damaging tissues.

Antioxidants came to the forefront when Linus Pauling, the two-time Nobel Prize winner, began advocating the use of the antioxidant vitamin C in high doses to prevent cancer and other diseases. Studies during the 1980s and 1990s began to confirm some of the benefits of these antioxidants, specifically vitamin C and vitamin E, in the prevention of colon cancer and heart disease, respectively. Countless companies began producing megavitamins with enormous doses of these antioxidant vitamins and supplements, basically stating that if some is good, then more must be better.

Is there any evidence that antioxidants can prevent or slow the development of osteoarthritis? Do you need to take them naturally, or do supplements provide similar benefits? Not all of the answers are clear, but you may find that eating foods with antioxidants may help. Studies from the Boston area over ten years ago found that patients who had diets high in vitamins C, D, and E had significantly fewer symptoms from their arthritis than patients who had diets that were low in these vitamins.

Numerous vitamins and minerals make up the antioxidants.

Vitamin A and Beta-Carotene

Vitamin A is necessary for maintenance of connective tissues. Vitamin A and its precursor, beta-carotene, are found in animal proteins, such as liver and eggs, as well as sweet potatoes, carrots, and leafy green vegetables, such as spinach. Although vitamin A and beta-carotene have numerous potential beneficial properties, taking too much can weaken bones and can lead to problems during pregnancy. Getting enough vitamin A without getting too much is essential for the health of your joints and surrounding tissues.

The B Vitamins

The B vitamins are actually a series of substances that have varying effects on the body. Although all are important in maintaining general health and well-being, a few have been discussed as potentially having a role in the prevention or treatment of osteoarthritis. Vitamin B_3, or *niacinamide*, has antioxidant properties and was purported to provide relief to patients with arthritis in one 1950s study, but little research (if any) has been done since that time on its effects. Vitamin B_5, or *pan-*

tothenic acid, was shown in one study in the 1960s to benefit patients with rheumatoid arthritis, but has not been studied in osteoarthritis. The same is true for the other B vitamins. Taking enough of the B vitamins is important for general health, but whether they have any beneficial effect on osteoarthritis is not clear.

Vitamin C

Vitamin C is essential for producing healthy collagen, a basic component of cartilage. Studies have shown that if you expose cartilage to vitamin C, more collagen forms in the joint. In animal studies, vitamin C, when added to the diet, improves cartilage health and subsequently helps to prevent osteoarthritis. Vitamin C is found most abundantly in citrus fruits, although bell peppers and cabbage also contain high amounts. It has been claimed that it boosts the immune system and helps prevent or lessen the effects of the common cold and other viruses if given in high doses.

The question is, how much vitamin C is too much—or is there such a thing as too much? Many people take massive doses of vitamin C to ward off a number of ailments. But there is little scientific evidence that megadoses of vitamin C work better than 500 to 1,000 milligrams per day. It is also unclear whether vitamin C obtained from a supplement works as well as vitamin C obtained from dietary sources. Although most people tolerate vitamin C well, it can upset your stomach and lead to kidney stones in susceptible individuals if too much is taken, so be careful. The benefits of vitamin C appear overall to clearly outweigh the risks.

Vitamin D

Vitamin D appears on the surface to have little to do with arthritis because its main effect is on bone, not cartilage. But we stated in the Introduction that the subchondral bone (the bone that lies directly underneath the cartilage of the joint) is crucial in providing the joint and its cartilage with the ability to absorb forces transmitted to the joint, as well as providing the cartilage with essential nutrients. If the bone below is not healthy, then the cartilage is likely not to be healthy as well. Vitamin D is necessary for the body to absorb and hold on to calcium, the building block of your bones. If you don't have enough vitamin D (and possibly if you have too much), your body doesn't absorb enough calcium and your bones become less healthy, including that important subchondral bone. Studies have clearly shown that people who had a higher intake of vitamin D had less progression of arthritis than people who did not.

Luckily, vitamin D is easy to get. Most people who walk outside during any part of the day will make enough vitamin D in their skin to meet their daily requirement. Drinking a glass of vitamin D–fortified milk (also a good source of calcium) or taking a regular multivitamin will provide you with the necessary 400 International Units (IU) per day. If you are over the age of sixty-five, you should probably take in closer to 600 to 800 IU per day because sometimes your body has a more difficult time converting vitamin D to its active form.

Vitamin E and Selenium

Vitamin E assists in maintenance of healthy joints and blood vessels. It works as an antioxidant and is present in nuts, spinach, asparagus, and unprocessed whole grains and vegetable oils. Taking high doses of vitamin E does not appear to provide any significant health benefit and can make mammograms more difficult to interpret.

Selenium may be necessary for vitamin E to be used effectively by the body. The amount of the mineral in your diet may depend on the amount in the soil where the grains you eat are grown. Certain types of fish, such as swordfish and salmon, contain selenium. It is thought to work in a fashion similar to omega-3 fatty acids by stimulating production of noninflammatory prostaglandins.

Boron

Boron is a naturally occurring substance contained in many of the foods that we eat. Some epidemiological studies indicate that people who live in areas where the boron content in foods is high may have a decreased risk of osteoarthritis. The potential explanations for this are varied and may have nothing to do with boron, but the subject piqued enough interest that the U.S. Department of Agriculture initiated a study to see whether controlling the amount of boron in the diet has any effect on the development or progress of arthritis.

Zinc

Zinc is another mineral that is an antioxidant. Studies have shown that people with rheumatoid arthritis generally consume less zinc than those without the disease. It is not clear whether zinc is protective against the development of rheumatoid arthritis or if supplementation of zinc will slow progression of the disease. Zinc may also work as a natural anti-inflammatory, but its role in the prevention or treatment of osteoarthritis is not well understood.

How Much of These Vitamins and Minerals Should I Take?

It's not entirely clear which exact quantities of which vitamins and minerals you should take, but one thing is certain: taking more is not necessarily a good thing. In fact, taking too much may be more dangerous to your health than not taking enough. To further complicate matters, the appropriate amounts may depend on your age and other factors. The following table offers some rough guidelines, but the absolutely perfect amount for any given person may vary. The doses recommended here should be safe, unless you have certain problems with your heart, liver, or kidneys (if you do, consult your doctor). The totals given in the table are from both daily food intake and supplements, so if you take in a large amount of a particular vitamin or mineral in your diet, you may need only a small supplement or none at all.

The table does not include all the vitamins and minerals you need to maintain a healthy and well-balanced diet, only those that *may* have some benefits in preventing or treating patients with osteoarthritis. Although none of the substances listed has been proven to protect joints, the potential benefits certainly make it worth giving them a try.

The Model Arthritis Diet

Is there such a thing as a perfect diet, one that will prevent or eradicate arthritis? Of course not. What may be the best diet for one person may not be best for another. Some people have or are at risk for arthritis because they are overweight, and a calorie-restricted diet may be more appropriate for them than for someone who is at a normal weight. Or you may have a medical condition that limits the types of foods you can eat. For instance, if you have diabetes, a diet loaded with fresh fruits may not be the right way to go.

In general, however, everyone can follow certain basic guidelines that will promote good health in general and good joint health in particular. It is important to remember that many of the concepts discussed in this chapter are not only good for your joints, but may be good for your heart, other organs, and blood pressure as well. The following recommendations are guidelines to help you make better choices about the types of foods you eat, how much to eat, and when to eat.

Vitamin or Mineral	Daily Recommended Dosage
Vitamin A (and beta-carotene)	5,000 IU
Vitamin B_3	500–1,000 mg
Vitamin B_5	250 mg
Vitamin C	500–1,000 mg
Vitamin D	400 IU
Vitamin E	400 IU
Selenium	100 mcg
Boron	1–3 mg
Zinc	15 mg

Your weight and activity level will largely determine the amount of calories you need and how closely you must monitor your caloric intake. If you are overweight, you will need to consume fewer calories than a person who is the same height but not overweight. In addition, if you are more physically active, you may be able to consume more calories than someone who is less physically active. Obviously, if you already have advanced arthritis, doing enough activity to lose weight may be a challenge. But you may find that if you can control your diet sufficiently, you can lose weight, taking pressure off your joints and allowing you to do more and burn more calories.

The type of food you eat is also important. The recommended ratio of carbohydrates to fats and proteins differs based on your caloric requirements. If you are limiting your calories, you also need to take care to minimize the percentage of fats in your diet while taking care to get adequate protein. The average American's diet is about 30 to 40 percent fat, but if you are significantly overweight your diet should be closer to 20 percent fat, possibly slightly lower.

Counting calories is not necessary for everyone. If your body weight is ideal and always has been, and you exercise regularly and are otherwise healthy, it's probably not necessary to count calories. You may find, however, that you are consuming too much fat and not enough protein or carbohydrates, and changing the types of foods you eat may offer significant health benefits.

In addition, the way you eat and the time of day you eat are important. Earlier in the day, your body needs fuel to carry out daily functions. Many people tend to skip breakfast, eat a "quickie" lunch, and then have a big late dinner. Although their caloric intake would seem appropriate for their body frame, they continue to be overweight. An old adage says, "Breakfast like a king, lunch like a prince, and dinner like a pauper." Eating the majority of calories earlier in the day when your body needs them most may go a long way toward helping you to reach your health goals, and you will probably think and feel better too.

How do you determine your ideal caloric intake?

1. Figure out your ideal body weight (see page 71 for formula).
2. Multiply by 13 to get the amount of calories you need each day if your activity level is low.

3. Add 20 percent if your activity level is moderate (exercising four to six hours per week); add 30 percent if your activity level is high (exercising more than six hours per week).

This should give you an approximate idea of how many calories it takes to maintain your ideal body weight. For example, a 5-foot, 4-inch woman with a normal frame who has an active job and exercises three to five times per week would calculate her ideal caloric intake as follows.

1. Ideal body weight is 120 pounds.
2. 120 pounds multiplied by 13 equals 1,560 calories.
3. Adding 20 percent for moderate activity, you get 1,560 + 312 = 1,872 calories to maintain ideal body weight.

Let's say, however, that the woman in this example weighs 160 pounds. She should decrease her intake by 20 percent (370 calories), and this should allow for weight loss of one to two pounds per week, which is a healthy rate at which to lose weight. Do not try to lose more quickly or limit calories more aggressively, as a certain number of calories in the correct proportion are necessary for good health and function. When you reach your ideal weight, you can go back to the recommended amount of calories.

What types of foods should you eat? Many of the foods discussed in this chapter that have been purported to protect your joints against damage and inflammation are those you should probably include in your list of healthy things to eat. Ensuring adequate intake of protein and fiber is essential, and limiting fat intake—especially saturated fats, which may help promote inflammation—is crucial. Generally, a good guideline to follow is to get the majority of your calories from carbohydrates (preferably whole-grain unrefined carbohydrates), fresh fruits and vegetables, and protein. If you are restricting calories in an attempt to lose weight, then limiting fat intake to ensure adequate protein intake is essential.

Avoiding processed sugars, candy, and snacks regardless of your caloric intake is crucial. And remember that when trying to adopt healthy eating habits, you should not burden yourself with hard-and-

Dietary Breakdown for Those Trying to Maintain Ideal Body Weight	
Carbohydrates	50–60%
Protein	20–25%
Fats	20–25%

Dietary Breakdown for Those Trying to Lose Weight	
Carbohydrates	50–60%
Protein	25–30%
Fats	15–20%

fast rules. It's fine to occasionally have ice cream or chocolate chip cookies. You should also try to change your eating habits gradually, not all at the same time, because you are trying to establish a basic lifestyle that you can maintain and enjoy long term that will promote health and well-being for your joints and the rest of your body.

A healthy diet is essential for the treatment and prevention of osteoarthritis. Maintaining an ideal body weight has been shown in study after study to reduce your risk and diminish the symptoms of this debilitating disease. In combination with a regular exercise program, good eating habits can help many people prevent or markedly reduce their symptoms of osteoarthritis. Unfortunately for some, this still may not be enough. Subsequent chapters will review the traditional and alternative medications now available to help prevent and treat osteoarthritis. However, the medications are effective only if you institute a program of diet and exercise that can reduce pain, increase function, and help you maintain or get back to a high level of activity.

Coping with Stress and Depression

Whether you are an athlete who has missed a few games with a twisted knee or a person with advanced arthritis who is frustrated about being unable to do the things you used to be able to do, stress, anxiety, and depression all can play a role in how you respond to injury and illness. It is natural to feel down when you hurt all the time, have difficulty doing activities that you used to take for granted, or can't play in the championship game. We all assume to one degree or another that we are invincible, and it's frustrating to face definitive proof that we aren't. Particularly when we are young, we rarely anticipate that one day we may not be able to walk up a flight of stairs without pain or make that diving catch on the softball field.

Although stress and depression may be normal responses to pain and injury, the way you deal with these emotions can determine how well you recover from injury. For instance, if you maintain a positive attitude after an injury, your recovery will almost certainly be quicker and more complete when compared to the recovery of someone who has a negative attitude. You not only will exercise harder and follow doctor's instructions more closely, but your positive state of mind can influence certain physiological responses that allow you to heal faster.

When you are under stress, your muscles can tighten or spasm. You might have noticed your neck feeling tense when you have had to deal with stressful situations in the past. Tight muscles can contribute to the pain and stiffness of osteoarthritis, and one of the goals of prevention and treatment is to loosen up the muscles so the joints can move more freely and be less prone to injury. In addition, stress, anxiety, and depression can through a variety of mechanisms increase your sensitivity to pain. Stress reduction can have a significant impact on muscle tone by reducing muscle spasms and improving flexibility, not to mention decreasing pain.

Joan is a forty-two-year-old woman who is a partner at a large law firm. About ten years ago, she hurt her back while working out. She went to her doctor, who recommended a short course of physical therapy and an exercise regimen, but because of her busy schedule she never followed through with the program. She never got over the pain in her back, and became discouraged by the fact that she had to modify her workout program, to the point that about a year ago she gave up on it altogether.

She began noticing about six months ago that she was more anxious than usual at work and at home, snapping at her partners and her kids. About three months ago Joan started feeling stiffness in her neck and shoulders, which she attributed to a stressful case she was working on. She finally went back to her doctor, who did x-rays and found that she had some early arthritic changes in her back and again recommended physical therapy and a home exercise program. Joan told the doctor that she had been under stress, and that she had gotten somewhat depressed about the pain and being unable to work out. Her doctor decided not to give her medication, but told her that she should consider a stress management program if things didn't improve.

Joan decided to attack the problem as if it were a tough legal case. She went to physical therapy and began a home stretching and strengthening program. She started adopting stress management techniques, including deep breathing, short rest breaks during the day, and focusing on maintaining a positive attitude toward her work and her pain. She began noticing improvement in her pain almost immediately and slowly became less grumpy. She has begun working out at the gym again, and although her back pain is not gone it has improved tremendously.

Reducing stress and anxiety and maintaining a positive attitude are crucial to any arthritis game plan. Many different techniques are available that can improve your outlook: meditation, massage, biofeedback, guided imagery, and even (in appropriate circumstances) medication.

Recognizing the Signs and Triggers of Stress

Stress can manifest itself in many forms, but some may be more obvious to you than others. For instance, if your neck and shoulders always get tight when you are on the freeway and caught in traffic, or if every time you have a big presentation you have to run to the bathroom three times before you start, it is clear that you are under stress. But sometimes the indications that you are suffering from stress are subtler. Signs such as short temper or forgetfulness may not be obvious to you. Here are just a few of the indicators that you are experiencing stress.

1. **Muscular tension.** Tightness in the neck and shoulders; headaches (usually in the back of the head or the temples); clenching your teeth, especially at night (sometimes known as *TMJ* or *bruxism*); aches in your back and/or neck

2. **Digestive problems.** Diarrhea, sometimes alternating with constipation; bloating; frequent heartburn; gas; intestinal spasms; stomach pains

3. **Heart symptoms.** Pounding in the chest or rapid heartbeat; chest pains (see your doctor if these recur to make sure you don't have a heart condition); palpitations

4. **Emotional symptoms.** Short temper; forgetfulness; difficulty sleeping; restlessness; irritability; frustration; feeling anxious; bad dreams

5. **Other symptoms:** Fatigue; increased use of alcohol or cigarettes

When you recognize that you have too much stress, how do you figure out what is causing it? Again, some things may be obvious to you, like too much work, or problems with your spouse or children. If you are having a tough time figuring out what is causing your stress, keeping a stress diary can be a big help. Write down all your activities during a given day and list how you feel while you are doing them. For example, if you start your day by taking a shower and eating breakfast, and you find those activities pleasurable, write that down. If you drive your kids to school and head off to work, and that leads you to feel short-tempered and anxious, write that down. Do this for a full

SAMPLE STRESS DIARY		
Time	**Activity**	**How I Feel**
7:30 A.M.	Wake up and take shower	Relaxed and slightly sleepy
7:45 A.M.	Eat breakfast and read newspaper	Relaxed
8:00 A.M.	Take kids to school	Anxious and rushed
8:30 A.M.	Drive to work	Increased stress when hitting traffic and running late
9:00 A.M.	Meet with staff to review daily schedule	Stress, too much to do today, mild stomach upset
9:15 A.M.	Prepare for presentation	Rushed, nervous
10:30 A.M.	Meeting with ad agency	Satisfied, meeting went well

week, including both weekday and weekend activities. You will be surprised at what stresses you out.

Stress is not all bad, and the way your body reacts to stress is a normal physiological phenomenon. For instance, stress increases blood flow to vital organs, including the brain, and improves concentration, which will come in handy if you have an important presentation to give. Stress helps you to get up for the big game and focus on what you need to do. This is so-called good stress. Stress becomes bad when it is more constant or occurs during situations when it is not necessary. That's when you begin to notice the symptoms we just described.

Once you figure out the causes of your stress, you can begin to manage it better. The simplest way to manage stress is to try to avoid or limit the activities that lead to stress, though this is much easier said than done (and sometimes not even possible). You may find that you are able to modify activities in a way that makes them less stressful. For instance, if you find you are always rushing in the morning to get the kids ready for school and get to work on time, you may want to wake up a few minutes earlier, or find a carpool for the kids so you are not in such a hurry. If a particular task at work causes you undue stress, try to get it done early so it doesn't weigh on your mind. This will allow you to get to the things you enjoy doing more, and keep you from dwelling on a task you dread. (Procrastination is a significant source of stress as well.)

Unfortunately, it is not always possible to eliminate the stresses in your life, especially if the inability to do your daily activities because of pain is one of the main sources of stress. You can, however, find alternative ways to diminish stress and the increased muscle spasms and pain that often accompany it. Here are some ideas you can use to lower your stress level.

1. **Deep breathing exercises.** Loosen any tight-fitting clothing. Place your hands on your stomach, close your eyes, and take a slow, deep breath in through your nose. You should feel your stomach pushing out. Blow out through your mouth slowly. You should now feel your stomach going in. Repeat a total of five times. This is a quick way to take your stress down a notch.

2. **Guided imagery.** Make sure you are in a quiet place. Loosen any tight-fitting clothing and sit in a comfortable chair. Close your eyes and imagine that you are in a place that you find relaxing and enjoyable, such as the beach or the mountains. Go to that place in your mind and stay for a few minutes. You will be surprised how relaxing it can be. If you can't be in a quiet place, you can take a "thirty-second vacation" in your chair at work or at home as well.

3. **Meditation.** Sit in a comfortable chair in a quiet place. Take a few slow, deep breaths. Close your eyes and remain quiet or repeat a meaningless sound over and over again for about fifteen to twenty minutes.

4. **Sleep.** Sleep is our most natural way of escaping stress. Unfortunately, when you are stressed or in pain, getting adequate sleep can be difficult. Trying to do relaxing activities before you go to bed can help you get a refreshing night of sleep and allow your battery to recharge. Also, when you are well rested, pain hurts less than when you are tired. Here are a few tips for healthy sleep.
   - Don't drink caffeinated beverages, except in the morning.
   - Eat meals with protein earlier in the day and carbohydrates at dinner. Carbohydrates provide only short bursts of energy, while protein has a longer-lasting effect.
   - Do not read or watch television in bed. Those activities can actually stimulate you and make it harder to fall asleep.
   - Do not nap for more than fifteen minutes during the day.

5. **Exercise.** Exercise is still one of the best ways to reduce stress, as well as being one of the keys to preventing and treating osteoarthritis.

6. **Massage.** Massages can help you to reduce stress and muscle spasms, but you need to incorporate other strategies that you can do on your own.

7. **Biofeedback.** Biofeedback is a technique that involves your "gaining control" over many of the so-called autonomic functions of your body, such as heart rate, breathing, muscle tension, and blood flow to the fingers. Certified biofeedback technicians can hook you to machines that measure all of these variables and teach you ways to reduce muscle spasms, slow heart rate, and increase finger temperature by increased blood flow (low finger temperature is a sign of decreased blood flow and increased stress levels). Through training, you can gain a level of control over these functions and find ways to diminish your stress response.

8. **Yoga.** Yoga is in some ways the original method of biofeedback. It incorporates many of the disciplines listed here to allow you to reach a more relaxed state. Yoga is not only an excellent source of relaxation, but can be a great way to exercise and get into shape.

9. **Avoid alcohol and other drugs.** Although alcohol and tobacco do help to decrease stress, the other stress reduction methods we've discussed are much more effective, are easily done at any time during the day, and do not have the potentially serious side effects of alcohol and tobacco. In addition, alcohol can disrupt normal sleep patterns.

There may not always be time for a massage or exercise during the middle of a busy day, but employing effective relaxation techniques can go a long way toward reducing stress and muscle spasms, and allow you to get back to doing the things you like to do.

Depression

You have noticed over the past several weeks that you have stopped calling your friends back and going out to dinner. You feel sad and tired all the time. You are constantly lamenting the fact that you can no longer do the stuff you need to do because of your arthritis pain. If this sounds familiar, you may be experiencing depression.

Depression is often referred to as an overall feeling of sadness that affects how you interact with the world. It can be mild or severe, and may be difficult to recognize when you are actually suffering from it. The dangers of depression include isolation, weight loss, increased risk of infections and other diseases, and even suicide. When you are depressed, you stop doing the things that can help you overcome the pain and stiffness of your osteoarthritis, and this actually can cause worsening of your symptoms.

How do you know if you or someone you care about is depressed? What are the symptoms? They include the following:

- Loss of interest in pleasurable activities
- Low energy level
- Decreased interest in sex
- Feeling sad or down much of the time
- Poor concentration
- Decreased memory and difficulty with decision making
- Increased or decreased sleep
- Change in appetite and weight
- Feeling guilty and dissatisfied about life

Other conditions, such as anemia and thyroid problems, can mimic depression. If you are experiencing these symptoms, go to your doctor to make sure that something else isn't going on.

It is normal if you are in pain all the time to have periods where you feel "down" about your condition. This is a typical response that most people have when they have a loss, be it the loss of a loved one or, in this case, the loss of ability to do certain activities. Trying to maintain a positive attitude is important in overcoming osteoarthritis, but having occasional bad days emotionally is to be expected. The down periods should concern you only if they are happening every day, or almost every day, for weeks at a time.

In most people depression is a treatable condition if it is recognized. For some, simply recognizing the signs allows one to change his or her attitude and address the problem. Some may require other types of help to get back on course. Some helpful support sources include the following.

1. **Support groups.** The Arthritis Foundation, your local hospital, and many others have support groups that meet on a regular basis. Often, simply being with others who are suffering with the same symptoms and hearing how they deal with them can benefit you, and the social interaction offered by these groups can also be of help.

2. **Counseling.** Speaking with a mental health professional, such as a psychologist, psychiatrist, or social worker, may be necessary. Most cities and many hospitals will have free or low-cost clinics that can provide good care if you don't have insurance to cover the expense. Ask your family doctor for a recommendation.

3. **Medications.** Numerous drugs have become available over the past ten to fifteen years that can help to treat depression with relatively few side effects. In addition, many of the medications in the antidepressant family have some pain-relieving benefits. Many people think that if they start taking an antidepressant they will be on it for life, but this is simply not true. Depression is often cyclical. In other words, people tend to have "down" periods of three to six months, after which they can often discontinue the medication. If you are unable to overcome the depression on your own, talk to your doctor about the options now available by prescription and over the counter.

Understanding the emotional reactions you have to your disease is crucial in overcoming the pain and stiffness of osteoarthritis. Stress, anxiety, and depression are commonly seen in patients with arthritis and other chronic illnesses. By recognizing the signs and symptoms, you can incorporate strategies into your arthritis game plan that will not only help to overcome the stress and depression that can go along with osteoarthritis, but allow you to continue on your path to beating this potentially debilitating ailment.

Traditional Therapies

What do you do when you have exercised diligently and lost weight and experienced some relief from arthritis symptoms, but you still suffer from the pain and stiffness of arthritis? Your joints ache less and you can move more freely, but you still can't open that jar of pickles and it still hurts to pick up your grandchildren. Finding that comfortable position in bed is still difficult and you don't sleep as well. Unfortunately, despite the best efforts, not everyone can overcome all the symptoms of osteoarthritis without some help.

The first two chapters have emphasized what *you* can do to help win the battle against osteoarthritis. Exercise, weight management, and healthy eating are crucial in overcoming the symptoms of arthritis and preventing its progression. Although these are the mainstays of treatment, when people have symptoms of pain that do not respond to exercise and diet alone, physicians will often recommend over-the-counter or prescription medications to help reduce pain and stiffness. Research into newer and safer therapies has revolutionized the way doctors treat arthritis. No one should have to suffer with pain any longer.

In "The Third Quarter" you will find:

- A review of medications currently available to arthritis sufferers, including the new COX-2 inhibitors—are these drugs the final answer in the war against osteoarthritis, or just hype?

- A discussion of what is coming in the future, including medications and methods that may actually help regrow cartilage.

Medications can be a necessary and effective part of a workable arthritis strategy. They can allow you to lead a more pain-free and active life.

Acetaminophen

Acetaminophen, most commonly know as Tylenol, has been one of the cornerstones of therapy to treat pain related to osteoarthritis. Acetaminophen works by inhibiting an enzyme that leads to pain. It doesn't reduce inflammation, but neither does it have the side effects, particularly stomach ulcers, of the traditional nonsteroidal anti-inflammatory drugs. Acetaminophen is safe and effective for many people in relieving the symptoms of osteoarthritis. A study conducted in the early 1990s showed that those who took 1,000 milligrams of acetaminophen four times a day (equivalent to two Tylenol Extra Strength tablets four times a day) experienced pain relief equal to that of people taking 800 milligrams of ibuprofen (such as Motrin or Advil) three times a day. Subsequent studies have questioned this and in fact suggest that anti-inflammatories are probably more effective. But if you have mild to moderate symptoms, acetaminophen may be a good and safe option.

Rarely, problems with acetaminophen have been seen. Among people who consume more than three alcoholic beverages per day, acetaminophen was associated with an increased risk of kidney and liver problems. People who take more than the maximum dose of 4,000 milligrams per day are at risk for significant liver toxicity, which can be fatal if not treated. For people who are generally healthy and consume alcohol only occasionally, acetaminophen is a safe and effective pain reliever.

Most people start taking acetaminophen on an as-needed basis using regular-strength pills (325 milligrams per pill), but you can take up to

4,000 milligrams per day if you do not have problems with your kidneys or liver. Anyone taking acetaminophen should not consume more than one alcoholic beverage per day. Acetaminophen is generally extremely well tolerated, and for many people it works well in relieving symptoms.

Topical Creams

Numerous over-the-counter pain relief creams have been available for many years to ease the pain and symptoms of arthritis. Common names for some of these creams include Mineral Ice, Bengay, Flexall 454, and Icy Hot, to name just a few. Topical patches have also been reported to relieve the symptoms of muscle and joint pain. The mechanisms for the pain relief these various agents offer are not entirely clear. Many of them provide a deep heating or cooling action to penetrate into the joint or muscle and provide relief. People often report that they feel better after using topical creams, but little scientific data (if any) supports these claims. The good news is that these topical agents have few to no side effects and can safely be used regularly.

For hundreds of years, Native Americans have used cayenne pepper to relieve pain in joints and muscles, grinding it up and rubbing it on the painful area. The pain would diminish for several hours. Scientists discovered that the ground cayenne pepper caused the nerve endings to release something called *substance P*. Substance P is found in nerves that are responsible for transmitting pain signals and is partially responsible for the perception of pain. The cayenne pepper would lead to a massive release of substance P from nerve endings, depleting it from the nerve. In the absence of substance P, the nerve is no longer able to transmit pain signals and pain is no longer perceived, even if it is present.

Pharmaceutical companies in the late 1980s adopted this ancient method and developed a medicinal-grade formulation called *capsaicin*, which was made available over the counter in the mid-1990s. The cream can be applied three to four times per day as needed depending on symptoms. It is often irritating and can cause redness and a burning sensation in the skin, which prevents many people from using it. The medication will last anywhere from three to eight hours, making frequent application a necessity. It works only on the joint you rub it on, so people with multijoint arthritis tend not to use it. There are no significant long-term risks to using capsaicin, but if you are going to give it a try, apply it at least one to two weeks before you give up on it.

Prescription creams and gels have also become more popular because of their high tolerability and low incidence of side effects. Creams and gels that contain traditional nonsteroidal anti-inflammatory drugs (common names for these include aspirin, ibuprofen, and naprosyn) are available through special compounding pharmacies. Compounding pharmacists can create a gel or cream that avoids many of the side effects of oral anti-inflammatories. It's not known how effective these creams are, although they have been available in Europe for several years. Clinical trials are going on in the United States at this time to determine their effectiveness.

Lidocaine gel and the new lidocaine patch work on a different mechanism. Lidocaine is closely related to novocaine, which is given to numb your mouth when you have a tooth pulled. It deadens nerve endings temporarily (one to two hours on average) when given via injection. Topical formulations are available, including a new time-release patch, which helps to overcome the limitation of the short duration of effect. Creams such as EMLA, which contains lidocaine and another longer-acting "caine," are also available by prescription. Patients can experience temporary relief of symptoms, but if multiple areas of the body are involved its usefulness is limited.

The main advantage of topical preparations is their tolerability and low side effects. Because the medications are only minimally absorbed, patients rarely experience any significant problems. The main drawbacks are that most need to be applied frequently, up to several times per day; and that they act only locally, relieving pain only in the area you rub the cream on. Rarely patients can develop rashes and skin irritation, especially to patches (due to the adhesive used). People who have arthritis in multiple joints will not likely find topical medications helpful. If you have a limited number of joints involved, a topical medication may be right for you.

Injections

Everyone has heard the story about the athlete who is injured during the big game, goes into the locker room for a "shot," and miraculously returns ten minutes later to lead the team to victory. Weekend warriors around the world have been looking for the magic shot that allows them to do whatever activity they want without feeling the soreness and pain that often accompany it. It would be wonderful if we had a shot that would instantaneously eliminate the pain of arthritis without harmful side effects. Unfortunately, medical science has not yet advanced to that level, but newer injections have become available that may help to significantly relieve pain from osteoarthritis.

The shots that athletes were given to allow them to get back into the game usually consisted of drugs like lidocaine, which essentially numbed the area of injury for one to two hours. The athlete paid the price later because the injury was not treated and the symptoms of the injury were masked. Lidocaine injections are rarely given today, as athletes risk more severe injury when they are unable to feel pain. Pain is your body's way of telling you when you shouldn't do a certain movement. Artificially overriding this mechanism is not only ineffective long term, but can be very dangerous.

The infamous "cortisone shot" has been available for decades and has been quite useful in patients who have pain in a particular joint. Rarely do doctors actually use cortisone; rather, they use other medications called *corticosteroids*. No, these are not the steroids bodybuilders use to increase bulk. Corticosteroids are your body's natural anti-inflammatories, and they have many important functions. When given at high concentration in injection or pill form, they can markedly reduce the swelling in a particular joint and reduce pain drastically for some patients. The shots are generally very safe if given appropriately, and can provide several months of pain relief for some.

Although inflammation is not a major component of osteoarthritis, the cortisone shot can still be of great benefit for people with arthritis. The greatest limitation of corticosteroid injections is that they don't always work. Steroids given long term by injection or pill are fraught with problems, including cataracts, diabetes, osteoporosis, and weight gain. When given in injection form on an occasional basis, however, these side effects are not seen and the injections can be given safely. Patient fears regarding steroids, despite their safety in this setting, will lead some to avoid this potentially beneficial option.

Significant publicity has been generated recently regarding the so-called "rooster mane" injections, medically known as *hyaluronic acid (HA) injections*. Hyaluronic acid is a normal constituent of healthy cartilage. When cartilage is worn down, HA is broken down, along with a number of other cartilage products. Injections of HA have been available outside the United States since the early 1990s and became available here in 1998. It is used only for osteoarthritis of the knee and is given in a series of three to five weekly injections. Studies are currently investigating whether patients with arthritis in the hip or shoulder might benefit from the shots. The injections are sold under the trade names Synvisc and Hyalgan.

The mechanism of action of hyaluronic acid injections is not entirely clear. Most likely, the injections act as a lubricant for the joint. When the joint is damaged by arthritis, the amount of synovial fluid decreases, leading to increased friction and pain within the joint, already roughened by the degeneration of the cartilage. *Viscosupplementation*, another word for HA injections, may increase joint lubrication, allowing the rough surfaces to glide over each other more easily, decreasing pain and stiffness in the knee. In addition, because hyaluronic acid is a natural constituent of cartilage, some think it may actually help to reconstitute cartilage and increase its thickness. For some patients, the injection may serve as an anti-inflammatory as well.

The injections are usually well tolerated, though some patients can get an intense inflammatory reaction, leading to pain and swelling of the knee. Although it is not dangerous, it can be extremely uncomfortable. Any time an injection is done, a small risk of infection exists, so the site needs to be monitored for signs of infection. Not everyone responds to the injections, and it is usually reserved for patients with advanced arthritis. Statistics show that it works about 50 percent of the time in patients with moderate to severe arthritis of the knee. It can be repeated every six months. Recent evidence indicates that patients with early arthritis may respond better, and for a longer period of time, than patients who have more severe arthritis. Patients who respond to the injection the first time will almost always respond to a further series of injections and will usually get even greater relief of their symptoms. Medicare and most major insurers cover the procedure, which can cost more than $500 for the series.

Injections with other substances, including glucosamine and chondroitin, have been studied, but none are presently available. If a doctor or alternative practitioner offers you another type of injection not mentioned here, be wary. The short- and long-term side effects may not yet be known and could lead to severe problems in the future.

Pain Medications

The main symptom of osteoarthritis is pain. The pain is what limits you from doing what you need to do. Although pain medications do not change the course of the disease, they may be necessary to allow patients with severe disease to function. Careful and judicious use of pain medications can provide substantial relief with limited side effects.

Tramadol, known as Ultram or, when combined with acetaminophen, Ultracet, is a pain reliever that does not act like narcotic pain relievers when taken in low doses. Four to six tablets a day may be taken to relieve pain. Rarely it causes drowsiness and upset stomach, but it is generally well tolerated. If given at higher doses, it can act like a narcotic pain reliever and does have addictive potential, so patients and doctors need to be careful about dosing. Tramadol does not cause ulcers, so people with a history of ulcers or heartburn can take it without concern about that.

Narcotic pain relievers come in many shapes and sizes. Common names include codeine, Darvocet, Vicodin, Percocet, OxyContin, and morphine. They are extremely effective in reducing pain, but have serious addictive potential. Given at low dose and only when needed, they can be a helpful addition to a treatment regimen when symptoms flare.

When given on a regular basis, people will often build tolerance to the drugs, requiring increasing doses to get relief. In addition, many people who take narcotic pain relievers develop nausea and severe constipation and become sleepy. Although there is a role for narcotics, the role is somewhat limited, and other avenues should be explored first.

Nonsteroidal Anti-Inflammatory Drugs

The most commonly prescribed class of drugs in the world is the nonsteroidal anti-inflammatory drugs (commonly called NSAIDs). Over 100 million prescriptions per year are written for these medications in the United States alone, and that represents only 10 to 20 percent of all of the NSAIDs taken, the majority being over-the-counter. NSAIDs are well known to most people by names such as aspirin, ibuprofen, Motrin, Advil, Naprosyn, Aleve, Voltaren, and Relafen. NSAIDs work by inhibiting an enzyme called *cyclooxygenase* that produces prostaglandins, which have wide-ranging effects. You might recall that prostaglandins are partially responsible for the pain and inflammation in patients with osteoarthritis. Unlike acetaminophen and narcotics, the NSAIDs not only relieve pain, but reduce inflammation as well.

NSAIDs are very effective in relieving the pain and stiffness associated with osteoarthritis, and have been the mainstay of therapy for many years. Arthritis patients who take NSAIDs say that they feel better and are able to go about their daily activities with greater ease. Recent studies have indicated that NSAIDs are more effective than acetaminophen in decreasing the pain of arthritis. People use NSAIDs not only for arthritis pain, but for other types of pain, including headaches, menstrual cramps, ankle sprains, and backaches. Over-the-counter NSAIDs are inexpensive and readily available in your local pharmacy or supermarket.

Of course, like most drugs, NSAIDs do have their downside. Prostaglandins have positive functions in the body: they protect the stomach lining against injury, help maintain blood flow to the kidney, and protect the function of platelets, allowing your blood to clot effectively. When you inhibit cyclooxygenase with a traditional NSAID, you diminish production of the "good" prostaglandins as well as the "bad" ones. The main negative effect is on the stomach; as the protective prostaglandins are decreased, ulcers can form and even bleed. In fact, in 1997, as many people died in the United States from ulcers caused by NSAIDs as died from AIDS!

A significant percentage of people who take NSAIDs complain about stomach upset, but this symptom does not necessarily indicate the presence of an ulcer. Most people who take NSAIDs think that if they do not have stomach upset they are exempt from getting ulcers. *Nothing* could be further from the truth. In fact, over half the people admitted to the hospital for a bleeding ulcer have no symptoms until they start hemorrhaging.

How do you know if you are at risk for a bleeding ulcer? Can we predict who will get this serious complication? The following are some factors that put you at greater risk for a bleeding ulcer:

- Age (older people are at higher risk)
- History of previous ulcer
- Poor health
- Regular use of corticosteroids (such as prednisone) for more than one month
- Use of two or more NSAIDs at the same time
- Use of blood thinners (Coumadin)

Overall, 1 to 2 percent of people who take an NSAID for one year will get a bleeding ulcer. Ten to 20 percent of patients on NSAIDs will develop stomach upset or heartburn, which are usually not related to ulcers and can often be treated easily. Switching NSAIDs can sometimes reduce symptoms. Over-the-counter antacids or H2-blockers (such as Tagamet, Zantac, Pepcid, and Axid) can often alleviate symptoms, but these drugs do not protect against ulcers.

Risks to the kidneys and liver are much smaller, but you should check with your doctor before taking any of these medications regularly, especially if you have ever had an ulcer or problems with your kidneys or liver. If you are going to have any medical procedure performed, even a simple dental procedure, do not take NSAIDs for a period of time prior to the procedure (see the table below). Remember, just because a medication is available over the counter does not mean that it is perfectly safe. No medication is truly "perfectly safe."

For the most part, these dangerous side effects can be prevented by medications given with NSAIDs. Unfortunately, these drugs can be costly and carry the risk of their own, albeit less serious, side effects. Misoprostol (Cytotec) is very effective in preventing ulcers, but causes

NSAID	Number of Days Before Procedure to Stop Taking Drug
Aspirin	10–14
Ibuprofen (Motrin, Advil)	1
Naprosyn (Aleve)	2
Ketoprofen (Orudis)	2
Relafen	3
Feldene	4
Diclofenac (Voltaren)	2
Indocin	2
Daypro	5

severe diarrhea in many patients. H2-blockers can reduce the stomach upset seen with NSAIDs but do not prevent ulcers.

Over the past two years, a revolution has occurred in the NSAID market with the advent of COX-2 inhibitors, the most successfully launched class of drugs in the history of the pharmaceutical industry.

COX-2 Inhibitors

In the late 1980s, scientists theorized that there may be two forms of the enzyme cyclooxygenase:

- COX-1, responsible for producing the prostaglandins that protect the stomach, kidneys, and platelets
- COX-2, produced only when pain or inflammation are present

Because the prostaglandins that trigger pain and swelling would be produced only when COX-2 was produced, the goal was to create an NSAID that would block COX-2 without blocking COX-1, theoretically gaining the benefits of the NSAIDs without many of the side effects (notably, bleeding ulcers).

The COX-2 enzyme was discovered in 1991 and pharmaceutical companies feverishly searched for agents that would selectively inhibit COX-2 while sparing COX-1. The result of this effort is the class of drugs we now know as *COX-2 inhibitors*. Four such agents have become available since 1999 in the United States: Celebrex, Vioxx, Bextra, and Mobic. (Mobic has been available in Europe since 1996 and is not officially listed as a COX-2 inhibitor in the Unites States, but is in Europe and most other countries.) The COX-2 inhibitors have become the most successful launch of any drug in history, generating U.S. sales of over $3.5 billion last year alone.

Is all the hype true? Are COX-2 inhibitors really "as safe as water," as has been claimed? Do they really prevent bleeding ulcers? And how might they fit into your strategy?

Doris is a seventy-three-year-old retired advertising executive who began noticing pain in her knees and fingers about two years ago. She had always been physically active, swimming, hiking, and going to aerobics classes three times a week for many years. When she was forty, she hurt her knees in a fall and started taking aspirin, but had to stop when she developed a small ulcer. She has always been slightly overweight, but she lost about twenty-five pounds when she started having pain. Her pain decreased some as she lost weight, but she continued to ache.

She tried to take Tylenol, but she did not get adequate pain relief. Doris began to get frustrated because she was having to limit her activities and couldn't take any NSAIDs due to her previous ulcer. When COX-2 inhibitors became available, she started taking one. She began noticing almost immediate pain relief and now is back to hiking and her aerobics classes, although now she takes a low-impact class.

Numerous studies have attempted to determine the safety of COX-2 inhibitors. The first studies on humans made use of *endoscopy*, a medical procedure in which a camera at the end of a long tube is inserted through the mouth into the stomach and intestines, allowing a view of the lining of these organs. If an ulcer or bleeding is present, the endoscope should show it. The studies showed that patients taking COX-2 inhibitors had ulcers approximately 5 percent of the time, compared to 20 to 40 percent of patients on the older NSAIDs. The striking discovery was that so many people on the older medications had ulcers, with some developing as soon as one week after starting the medication. Thankfully, most of these ulcers don't bleed, but one can develop serious bleeding if the ulcer digs a hole into a blood vessel.

Studies began investigating whether COX-2 inhibitors actually prevent bleeding ulcers, which kill 16,500 people each year and cause more than one hundred thousand people in the United States to be hospitalized. It was discovered that patients who take COX-2 inhibitors lower their risk of developing bleeding ulcers by about 50 percent when compared to the older NSAIDs. Why not 100 percent, or at least close to that figure? The answer is quite simple: some people get ulcers whether they take anti-inflammatories or not. Not all ulcers are caused by anti-inflammatories, and therefore some people, regardless of how safe the newer agents are, will get ulcers for a completely unrelated reason. The bacterium helicobacter pylori has been linked to ulcers not caused by NSAIDs and is the most common cause of bleeding ulcers other than NSAIDs.

So are the COX-2 inhibitors really "as safe as water?" Probably not, if for no other reason than the fact that no drug is as safe as water. All COX-2 inhibitors do inhibit the COX-1 enzyme to some degree, even if small, and in patients who are sensitive this may be enough to lead to a bleeding ulcer, however rarely. COX-2 inhibitors can have the same effects as the older medications, so you may not be able to take them if you have problems with your kidneys or liver. All NSAIDs, new or old, can lead to fluid retention, which in turn causes swelling in the legs (although the swelling reverses when you stop the medication). Anywhere from 1 to 3 percent of patients can get swelling, and the percentage on one of the newer agents may be even higher. There has also been controversy of late over suspicion that one of these newer drugs may actually cause heart attacks and raise blood pressure. However, this suspicion is by no means proven, and more studies are being conducted to investigate it.

The selective COX-2 inhibitors do not regrow your cartilage. They are also significantly more expensive than many of the regular anti-inflammatories, costing two to four dollars a day. But they are very effective in treating pain and stiffness related to arthritis, and can improve function and quality of life for many arthritis sufferers. Even though they may not be "as safe as water," they markedly reduce the most serious and deadly complication of NSAIDs.

The major pharmaceutical companies are continuing to develop newer and possibly safer COX-2 inhibitors. Whether the perfect agent can be produced remains to be seen. In the past, we used to tell our older patients to take their NSAIDs only when they really needed them, to avoid developing bleeding ulcers. With the newer agents and their improved safety, we now can tell patients to take their drug on a regular basis, affording them better pain relief and increased function. The medications taken at full regular dose may also help to reduce inflammation, leading to better pain control and decreased stiffness in the joints.

The COX-2 inhibitors have opened the door for many arthritis sufferers who were either afraid or unable to take any of the traditional anti-inflammatory medications, and they have given doctors another weapon in the war against osteoarthritis. They are not the final answer, but they are definitely a major step forward.

Diacerein

Diacerein was originally approved for the treatment of osteoarthritis in France in 1992 and has been more recently approved in several other countries. It is thought to reduce inflammation, decrease the breakdown of cartilage, and stimulate the production of new cartilage. It works differently than NSAIDs, as it does not inhibit prostaglandins. Recent studies have shown it to be effective in reducing the pain and stiffness associated with osteoarthritis, and theoretically it may help to slow the loss of cartilage. Studies have not yet been done in the United States, but if evidence of this drug's effectiveness is found, you may see in the next few years a new weapon in the war against this disease.

Metalloproteinase Inhibitors

Metalloproteinases and *collagenases* are enzymes that are partially responsible for the breakdown of cartilage once it has been damaged. In theory, a medication that blocks the actions of these enzymes should prevent the breakdown of cartilage. Pharmaceutical companies have been working to develop medications that can safely and effectively do just that. Research studies in patients with osteoarthritis have begun, and the hope is that these medications will live up to their promise. Unfortunately, it may be some years yet before we know.

Tetracyclines

Tetracyclines are a group of antibiotics that have been around for decades and treat a wide variety of infections. Over the last decade, tetracylines (known under such names as Minocin, Vibramycin, Doxycycline, and Sumycin) have been shown to inhibit some substances that cause inflammation as well as some of the metalloproteinases. In fact, Minocin is being used in patients with mild rheumatoid arthritis, although the results have been mixed. Studies are now reviewing the potential therapeutic role of tetracyclines in the treatment of osteoarthritis. The extremely low cost and minimal side effects of these drugs make them an attractive possibility if it is found that they are effective against osteoarthritis.

Heat and Cold

Many people seem not to know, or perhaps simply forget, how effectively heat and cold reduce the symptoms of osteoarthritis, and at a minimal cost. Cold therapy reduces swelling from acute injuries and alleviates pain, especially if you have had a recent flare-up of symptoms. Use of cold in the first forty-eight hours after injury can markedly reduce inflammation and decrease discomfort. If you have chronic joint problems, ice "massage" can help to diminish pain in joints that are flaring up. Fill several three-ounce paper cups with water and put them in the freezer. When your joint pain increases, take a cup out and peel off the paper on the outside. Roll the ice over the joint for about fifteen minutes. Repeat every couple of hours. You can also use a bag of frozen vegetables, as it easily molds to your body.

Heat can decrease muscle spasms and loosen up chronically stiff and painful joints. A hot shower or soak in a warm bath can bring welcome pain relief and relaxation. Hot packs can be applied to particular areas of stiffness, but should be left on no longer than fifteen minutes at a time. If you use a heating pad, never fall asleep on it, as it can lead to serious burns. Paraffin wax treatments, which involve dipping your hands or feet in a hot wax preparation, can also provide significant relief of symptoms.

Bracing

The use of braces to treat or prevent arthritis is far from new. Bracing involves providing additional support to joints and muscles via an external device, thereby preventing or reducing the risk of damage to the joint, or decreasing pain if the joint is already damaged.

People have worn back braces for years to help deal with back pain, although there is little evidence (if any) that a simple corset actually helps reduce pain. In fact, most doctors do not recommend back braces for pain relief, as evidence seems to suggest that the braces may actually delay recovery from injury and lead to weakness of the back muscles. Back braces are often used after surgery to prevent the patient from moving in ways he or she shouldn't, or to protect the back against injury when doing heavy lifting. However, back braces should probably not be used for chronic back pain.

Braces for other parts of the body may be more helpful. In the 2002 Winter Olympics, many of the athletes on the U.S. ski team wore knee braces, not because they had knee injuries, but because of the high risk of joint damage while going at high speeds through turns and over moguls. The braces help to support the ligaments of the knee and prevent injury. Knee braces can be quite helpful in preventing joint damage. If you already have arthritis, some knee braces can help you "unload" the area of the joint that is problematic. In other words, the brace can take the pressure off the part of your cartilage that has suffered the most damage and allow your joint to move more freely and with less pain. Arthritis in the first CMC joint (the joint at the base of your thumb) can be relieved greatly by a form-fitting brace molded by an experienced hand therapist, and orthotics can significantly reduce pain in your feet related to joint deformities. By transferring or absorbing some of the force that would normally be placed on an arthritic joint, you can significantly reduce symptoms and gain function.

Liquid Cartilage

Despite the newer and safer treatments now available, nothing as of today cures osteoarthritis. Researchers are continuing to search for drugs that may actually preserve cartilage or even regrow it. Lab techniques now exist whereby new cartilage can be grown in liquid form (from old cartilage); the new cartilage is essentially injected into an area of deficit, healing the cartilage. A small piece of bone is used to cover the liquid so it doesn't leak out and the cartilage is then filled in, fixing the problem. Unlike medication or older surgeries, the cartilage is actually restored to normal, preventing or reversing the arthritic process. The procedure is done through an arthroscope and is considered minor.

Is this "the cure"? For technical reasons, unfortunately, this technique can benefit only a very small number of osteoarthritis patients, maybe less than 1 percent. Unless there is a very clear tear or hole, the liquid will leak out and will not restore the deficit. However, one can imagine the day that this technology may be used for a broader spectrum of arthritis sufferers and may actually return the cartilage to a normal, healthy state. Researchers are looking for new ways to apply this technology beyond its currently limited uses.

Surgery

You're exercising religiously, you've lost weight, you're taking a selective COX-2 inhibitor, and yet you hurt. Your knee aches and creaks and you can't climb a flight of stairs or get out of your car. The pain prevents you from getting a good night's sleep, and you can't bend down to pick up your granddaughter. Unfortunately, despite your best efforts, you now have an appointment with an orthopedic surgeon to discuss the options for surgery.

Two common surgeries are performed on patients with osteoarthritis: *arthroscopy* and *joint replacement*. Surgeons perform an arthroscopy by placing a small scope into the joint (usually the knee) and viewing the inside of the joint on a video screen. Through the scope and its instruments, the surgeon can repair tears in the cartilage, shave down rough surfaces to make them glide across one another better, and flush the joint, presumably removing debris, crystals, and substances triggering inflammation. Unfortunately, some recent studies have found that arthroscopy does *not* help with symptoms from osteoarthritis of the knee. Neither the small joints of the hands and feet nor the hip are amenable to this procedure. In addition, when you smooth the cartilage, you are actually removing healthy tissue from an area that already has little cartilage to spare. Arthroscopy is usually a bridge to provide symptom relief until a more definite treatment is performed.

Joint replacement is the method of last resort. When all else has failed, metallic joints can replace arthritic joints in the knees, hips, and shoulders. Options are available, but limited, for other joints. The diseased cartilage is removed, along with the surrounding structures, and the new joint is inserted. The new joints can last up to ten to fifteen years, and the pain is greatly reduced—sometimes even eliminated. For patients with advanced disease, this can be the difference between walking and using a wheelchair.

Joint replacement surgery is much more substantial than arthroscopy, and requires weeks to months of rehabilitation. Complications can occur, including bleeding, blood clots, and infection. Many patients who require joint replacements can have other medical problems that make surgery more risky. All options should be considered prior to pursuing joint replacement.

Is the Cure on the Horizon?

Scientists are actively involved with numerous projects that may eventually offer the answer for patients who suffer from osteoarthritis. Enhanced understanding of the mechanisms of the destruction of cartilage have allowed researchers to try to pinpoint more specific therapies directed at the causes of arthritis. New therapies are targeting the enzymes that lead to the destruction of cartilage. The difficulty is that many of these enzymes are present in many different organs and cells in the body, and can affect other areas than the ones we desire.

Gene therapists are looking at ways to insert new DNA into the cells that produce cartilage and its matrix in hopes of turning these cells on or modifying their behavior so that they make cartilage rather than destroying it. Understanding of the genes that trigger premature osteoarthritis will allow scientists to figure out what these genes are doing and target therapy more directly. The future is bright with options, but none is expected within the next few years.

How Does All of This Fit into Your Strategy?

You know the importance of diet and exercise to overcome the pain and disability of osteoarthritis, and you now have a good understanding of the options available if exercise and diet are not enough. Even if you choose to use one or more of the options presented in this chapter, diet and exercise are still the key. Study after study has demonstrated the benefits of joint-specific and general conditioning exercises for not only your joints, but your heart as well. If you and your doctor decide that medication is right for you, that does not absolve you from the need to exercise and maintain a healthy weight.

The safest options should be considered first, although no medication is "as safe as water." Discussing these matters with your doctor is essential in deciding which option is right for you. You need to take into account any medical problems that you might have prior to starting any medication.

Medication can also serve as a bridge, reducing pain and stiffness to the point that you can begin exercising. Then, as strength improves and joints become more limber, you can decrease or stop the medication. Avoiding medication is always best when possible, but you shouldn't suffer with pain when safe and effective pain-relief options are available.

A comprehensive program requires communication between you and your doctor. Before embarking on an exercise regimen or diet program, or taking an over-the-counter medication, you should formulate a strategy with your doctor. You can win the war against osteoarthritis, but it takes work and perseverance. You are your best weapon in this war.

"Working Overtime" will review the role of all four quarters and help you to set up your arthritis strategy.

Alternative Therapies

If you watch television or read magazines, you would think that the cure for arthritis is already here. Be it glucosamine and chondroitin, MSM, SAM-e, or the latest berry from the juniper bush found only on the island of Madagascar, claims of the miracle cure for arthritis abound. You have suffered with pain for years, or have watched a friend or family member struggle with osteoarthritis and want to avoid the same outcome. You are willing to try anything to move without pain. But how do you know if what they are saying is true? How do you know whether these, or one of the various herbs or other "natural" remedies, really work? Information is often lacking, and attempting to research it on your own can be a daunting task.

In "The Fourth Quarter" we will try to give you the most up-to-date information on the various alternative therapies presently on the market. You will find that some of these remedies really do have a scientific basis for their claims to improve or prevent the symptoms of osteoarthritis. Others rely on folklore and testimonials in place of evidence to convince you that their "cure" is the true arthritis cure.

The greatest difficulty in looking at these alternative therapies is that none of them has gone through the rigorous scientific analysis that is required before a traditional medication is approved to go on the market. The U.S. Food and Drug Administration (FDA) requires that a traditional pharmaceutical be put through a series of studies to ensure its safety and efficacy. The arduous process of performing numerous basic and clinical trials takes several years, often costing a pharmaceutical company tens or even hundreds of millions of dollars before a medication is allowed onto the U.S. market. Similar processes and agencies exist in other countries as well. Although mistakes are made and drugs occasionally reach the market without all of the dangers coming to light, the process usually definitively establishes the effectiveness of a medication and reveals its side effects, which are deemed to be reasonable based on the potential benefit of the medication. This is not to say that traditional medications are necessarily safe; actually, many are not. It means that the benefits of the medication outweigh the risk, based on scientific analysis. In any case, before starting any medication, you and your doctor need to work together to ensure that the medication makes sense for you.

Consider some of the newer drugs used to treat high cholesterol—Lipitor, Zocor, Pravachol, Mevachor, and Lescol. Studies have shown that certain groups of patients taking these medications can lower their risk of a heart attack by 20 to 50 percent. However, there is an approximately 1 percent risk of having an elevation of your liver function tests or muscle enzymes, possibly leading to pain and weakness. The FDA appropriately decided that the benefits (lowering cholesterol and subsequently the rates of heart attack) well outweighed the risk of a usually reversible problem in the liver and muscles, and established guidelines for monitoring the potential side effects of these medications.

No such standard exists for alternative medications. They are not monitored by regulatory agencies in the same way and therefore do not have to go through the same rigorous scrutiny that traditional medications do. With the costs of performing such studies often prohibitive to smaller manufacturers, less research is done to determine potential benefits and risks. Some of the alternative agents, such as glucosamine and chondroitin, have now been studied in several well-done, albeit smaller, trials; glucosamine and chondroitin are actually the subject of a large government-funded study at this time. Others, however, have little or no scientific evidence to back up their claims.

But remember lack of proof of efficacy does not mean proof of lack of efficacy. In other words, even if the scientific evidence appears to be lacking, that does not prove that a medication does not work. Although people have used glucosamine and chondroitin for many years, often despite the objections of their skeptical physicians, it is only recently that we have begun collecting evidence of the potential benefits of these drugs. Acupuncture has been around for close to three thousand years without any controlled scientific data. If you have ever had acupuncture and it has helped, someone would be hard put to convince you that just because science hasn't figured out exactly why it worked, that it was all in your head (and, presumably, millions of other people's heads as well). And even with traditional medication, doctors often use the drugs for conditions and in ways that were never reviewed by the FDA. So even if an alternative treatment has not undergone the intense scientific scrutiny of a traditional pharmaceutical, it could still help your symptoms.

"The Fourth Quarter" will attempt to help you sort out fact from fiction and show you where some of these alternative therapies might fit into your arthritis game plan. If you are an educated and informed consumer, you may find that some of these therapies make sense for you, and you can avoid putting yourself at risk or spending hundreds, maybe even thousands, of dollars on a wish and a prayer.

General Guidelines

Because the alternative therapy market is not closely regulated, your chances of getting fleeced are greater. Unlike traditional medications, herbs and other natural remedies may not contain the actual ingredients they claim to. Ten years ago a study showed that about half of all herbal and natural remedies did not contain what they claimed to contain on the bottle, and in some cases contained toxic substances. With that in mind, here are some general rules you can use to protect yourself from harm and give yourself the best chance to benefit from these remedies.

1. Make sure you buy your products from a reputable source. Many major companies and chains are now in the alternative therapies business. The more established manufacturers have for years used standards of quality control to ensure that their products contain what they say they contain, and they usually use high-quality ingredients. Although a practitioner who makes the compounds may be as good as or even better than a bigger company, just be careful.

2. Know what your medical problem is so that you buy the right stuff. I can't tell you how many times I have had patients buy glucosamine and chondroitin for conditions other than arthritis and then not understand why it isn't working. Just like traditional medications, no one therapy cures everything.

3. Check the label. Make sure you are getting what you think you are getting and in the correct dosage, as often the claim on the front of the bottle doesn't match the list of ingredients on the back of the bottle.

4. Take the medication as prescribed and for as long as recommended to see an effect. If you are going to try one of these therapies, give it a fair shot. For instance, you need to take glucosamine and chondroitin for at least two months for it to have an effect. Many people give up on a drug, be it traditional or alternative, after just a few days. They'll never know if it might have helped.

5. If you have other underlying health problems, check with your doctor before you try anything. Just as traditional medications can interact with one another, so can alternative therapies. Don't just mix and match as you see fit.

6. If you have any side effects, report them to your doctor immediately and discontinue the medication. The word "natural" on a label does not guarantee that the product is safe.

So, is the miracle cure really out there, something that can get rid of the pain for good?

Glucosamine and Chondroitin

You have heard about them on the news, in coffee shops, on TV talk shows, and even in your doctor's office. Glucosamine and chondroitin came to the national forefront in 1997 when Jason Theodosakis, Brenda Adderly, and Barry Fox released the book *The Arthritis Cure*. They stated that among those who took glucosamine and chondroitin regularly, "the vast majority of patients with osteoarthritis will get significant relief and may avoid the harmful effects of many standard treatments offered by the current medical system." Patients looking for an answer bought the supplements by the truckload, despite the concerns of many in the medical community that there had not been enough testing to prove that these agents worked.

Norma is a seventy-one-year-old retired secretary who has suffered with pain in her knees for several years. She went to see her doctor, who did an x-ray and diagnosed her with osteoarthritis. She started an exercise program and healthy eating plan to help her lose twenty pounds. After about three months, she had lost five pounds and felt that her pain had decreased by about a third. She continued to have difficulty getting in and out of chairs and had pain when she walked.

She was reluctant to take the prescriptions that her doctor had recommended, so after consulting with her doctor she decided to try glucosamine and chondroitin. After about four weeks, she began noticing decreased pain and stiffness; after three months, she could get in and out of chairs more easily and could walk farther without pain. She continues to take the supplements a year later in hope that it might help to regrow her cartilage.

Glucosamine and chondroitin are natural constituents of cartilage, so it is thought that giving them as supplements will help stimulate cartilage to regrow, reversing the process of arthritis. In other words, taking these so-called building blocks of cartilage will increase production of the other substances in cartilage, eventually resulting in less pain and stiffness.

But some were suspicious initially, for a couple of reasons. First, the patients who respond to glucosamine and chondroitin usually do so within about two to three months, which seems an unreasonably short period in which to restore years of damage to joints. Second, it was believed that glucosamine and chondroitin would be broken down by the stomach acid and digestive juices and therefore never get to the joints. However, a recent study using a very sophisticated technique showed that not only was the majority of the glucosamine and chondroitin being absorbed into patients' systems, but that up to 70 percent of the glucosamine and chondroitin actually makes it to the joints.

Does the fact that these substances make it to your joints confirm that they actually work? Not necessarily, but it is a start. The fact that many patients note relief within a few weeks implies that glucosamine and chondroitin have another mechanism to help with the symptoms of osteoarthritis. Is it a placebo effect? That is, do people just convince themselves they feel better, when it is actually no more effective than a sugar pill? Based on recent research, the answer is probably no. In fact, numerous studies now seem to imply that taking glucosamine and chondroitin is better than taking a placebo in relieving the pain and stiffness of osteoarthritis, and two recent well-done studies imply that it may even help to preserve cartilage.

A recent study from Belgium studied over three hundred patients with osteoarthritis and found that patients taking glucosamine and chondroitin over two years had less pain and stiffness than patients taking a placebo. More interesting, the patients who took the supplements did not lose any cartilage during the two years, while the patients who got the placebo lost an average of 0.4 millimeters of cartilage (approximately one-sixtieth of one inch). Although the amount of cartilage lost was minimal, this finding does imply that glucosamine and chondroitin have a protective effect on cartilage. The National Institutes of Health is presently sponsoring a study that will be by far the largest and best study done to date on the potential pain-relieving and cartilage-protective effects of glucosamine and chondroitin. The study is reviewing 1,800 patients with osteoarthritis of the knee, and we hope that it will help to settle any remaining questions about the benefits of these two substances.

To date, not a single study has shown that glucosamine or chondroitin can increase the amount of cartilage you have in your joints, although it appears that they help to prevent further loss of cartilage. If you do not treat osteoarthritis, over time you will likely continue to slowly lose cartilage, which can lead to increasing pain and stiffness. It does appear that in some patients glucosamine and chondroitin help to reduce the pain and stiffness of osteoarthritis and may even prevent or at least slow down its progression. At minimum they probably act as some sort of natural anti-inflammatory pain reliever, accounting for that relief you may feel within a couple of months of starting the medications.

So, are glucosamine and chondroitin for everyone? How are they taken? If you and your doctor agree that you are a candidate for glucosamine and chondroitin, remember that results are not immediate. You have to give it at least two months to see if the combination works before you give up on it. With the cost of most of the supplements running anywhere from twenty to sixty dollars a month, you could put out a lot of money.

The average person should start with 1,500 milligrams of glucosamine and 1,200 milligrams of chondroitin per day. If you are very thin (less than 110 pounds or 50 kilograms), you may want to decrease to 1,000 milligrams of glucosamine and 800 milligrams of chondroitin; if you are heavy (more than 220 pounds or 100 kilograms), you may want to go up to 2,000 milligrams and 1,600 milligrams, respectively. These rules are not hard and fast, as the ideal dosages are still not known with certainty.

Most people tolerate glucosamine and chondroitin well. If you have a history of diabetes or glucose intolerance, you probably should not take glucosamine, as it can increase your blood sugar. Other side effects are rare, and most people can take these products without any difficulty.

So, where do glucosamine and chondroitin fit into your arthritis game plan? Some suggest that glucosamine and chondroitin work better on osteoarthritis of the knees than in other parts of the body, although I have never heard any reasonable explanation as to why that would be the case. If you already have osteoarthritis and don't have diabetes, and exercise and diet changes don't seem to offer enough relief, then it may be worth giving them a try. As always, talk to your doctor first.

What if you don't have osteoarthritis, but are active, overweight, or have a strong family history of arthritis, and want to try to prevent the development of arthritis? Is there any evidence that you can stop arthritis before it starts by using these two supplements? No studies to date have investigated this issue, so at this time it is unclear whether these products may be effective preventive agents. As with any medication or supplement, it is important to remember that no drug is completely safe.

MSM, SAM-e, DMSO, and Other Sulfur Compounds

Sulfur is an element that is normally contained in the cartilage. Animal studies have shown that the concentration of sulfur in arthritic joints is only one-third of that in healthy joints, leading to the proposed supplementation of this element. Some have theorized that the sulfur molecule, if given in high concentrations via foods or natural supplements, can work as a natural anti-inflammatory and help to reconstitute cartilage. Some even postulate that glucosamine is effective not because it is a specific component of cartilage, but because it contains sulfur. Garlic, which many have touted as nature's healer, contains a high concentration of sulfur, but no well-done study to date has demonstrated any specific benefit of garlic in arthritis.

Around 1999, actor James Coburn brought *MSM (methylsulfonylmethane)* to public attention when he began touting it as the magical remedy that helped reduce his arthritis pain, and the book *The Miracle of MSM* led to skyrocketing sales of this supplement. The potential benefits of MSM are reported to be many, including decreased transmission of pain signals in nerves, reduction of muscle spasms, increased blood flow to joints and muscles, and a decreased rate of cartilage breakdown. Some claim that if you have arthritis you are naturally low in MSM, and therefore replenishing your body's stores of this compound will reduce pain and swelling from arthritis. A couple of smaller studies in patients with rheumatoid arthritis report some potential benefits, but these studies have not been confirmed. In fact, there is little scientific evidence (if any) to support the use of MSM in osteoarthritis, and in my experience most patients see little or no relief with MSM. In the literature that is most favorable to alternative remedies, many agree that the reported benefits of MSM are based only on testimonials by a small number of people, not on scientific study.

DMSO (dimethyl sulfoxide) is another source of sulfur and has been used as an industrial solvent for years. It has effects as a so-called "transporter" or "carrier" substance. In other words, it helps other products to penetrate through the skin and get absorbed more easily. The evidence of any benefit in arthritis is sketchy at best, and there are reports of potential damaging effects on the nervous system. Without strong scientific proof of results and possibly dangerous side effects, you need to be very careful if you are thinking about trying DMSO.

SAM-e (S-adenosylmethionine) is a sulfur-containing compound that naturally binds with a substance in your body called ATP and is involved in a number of bodily functions. SAM-e has been used in other countries for years as an antidepressant, and has been discussed as a natural pain reliever and anti-inflammatory since the 1980s. A number of studies from Europe that were published in a single supplement to the *American Journal of Medicine* in 1987 stated that SAM-e was just as effective and safe as prescription NSAIDs for up to six weeks in the treatment of the symptoms of osteoarthritis. Other than this one issue of one journal, however, few studies, if any, confirm or deny these findings, and none to date look at SAM-e for a longer period of time.

SAM-e seems to be fairly well tolerated when given for two to four weeks at doses up to 400 milligrams two to three times per day, then decreasing to 400 milligrams per day. It can cause an upset stomach, which usually resolves when the medication is stopped. If you are going to try SAM-e, it is important to remember that there are no long-term studies to determine whether it is safe or effective—and osteoarthritis is a long-term problem, not a short-term problem. Also, SAM-e can be expensive, up to a hundred dollars per month, which is more costly than the new, safer COX-2 inhibitors. And there is no evidence that they protect your cartilage. So you can try SAM-e, but your money may be better spent on a COX-2 inhibitor.

Cetyl Myristoleate

In the early 1960s, a researcher for a branch of the National Institutes of Health by the name of Dr. Harry Diehl discovered that a certain type of mouse seemed to be immune to the development of arthritis when given experimental substances that would normally cause arthritis. After years of research, he reportedly identified an agent known as *cetyl myristoleate*, an oil that might be responsible for the resistance to arthritis seen in these animals. It is thought that this substance may work as a natural anti-inflammatory because it is in the family of omega-3 fatty acids (discussed in the Second Quarter), but may have longer-lasting benefits than omega-3 fatty acids found in standard dietary sources. Although exact replication of the oil has been difficult, companies have been trying to develop similar compounds that potentially would benefit patients with arthritis. Numerous companies have synthesized substances that closely resemble cetyl myristoleate and have touted its miraculous effects on patients who suffer from many forms of arthritis, not just osteoarthritis.

Unfortunately, as is the case with many of these natural remedies, the lack of scientific evidence to support its use is striking. Although testimonials exist claiming miraculous results in a short period of time with minimal side effects, only two studies of actual patients were done, and these included a relatively small number of patients with osteoarthritis. In fact, *The Quarterly Review of Natural Medicine* in 1997 stated that CMO (the most common commercially available derivative of cetyl myristoleate) "remains an expensive (though apparently safe) experiment" and that the studies on its efficacy up to that time "would not have been published in its current form by a normal peer-reviewed journal" (Austin 1997, 315–16).

As this substance is similar to fish oil, bloating, gas, and diarrhea are the most commonly reported side effects. The recommended total dose is 12 to 15 grams in divided doses over one month, or about 500 milligrams per day. It is suggested that you take the pancreatic enzyme lipase with it, as it can be difficult to digest because of its oily nature. However, it is important to remember that as of now, the scientific evidence of CMO's safety and benefits in osteoarthritis is not yet available, so if you choose to try it, do so with caution.

Emu Oil

In the early 1990s, reports surfaced about Australian Aborigines rubbing the fat of emu birds on their joints to reduce pain and inflammation. Emus are indigenous to Australia, but emu farms began sprouting up all over Texas based on this and on reports that emu meat tasted like beef, but with much lower saturated fat content. Emu oil was produced as a potential natural anti-inflammatory and pain reliever. Unfortunately, the results were not as positive as had been hoped, and without studies to support its use and with a price tag of about twenty dollars a bottle, emu oil never was embraced by the American public. I'm sure, however, that if you wanted to you could pick up an emu really cheap right now as a pet.

Other Herbal and Dietary Remedies

A variety of other herbs have been advanced as natural anti-inflammatories over the years. These include such compounds as boswellia, feverfew, white willow bark, sea cucumber, turmeric, wheat grass, green lipped mussels, and ginger, just to name a few. Many of these substances have been used for hundreds, if not thousands, of years to help reduce the pain and inflammation related to osteoarthritis. Although the depth of scientific research for most of these herbs is minimal, you may be surprised to find that some of them have some potential to help you reduce the pain and stiffness in your joints.

Turmeric (Curcumin)

Turmeric, a spice derived from the turmeric root, has been used in India for centuries in curry, but has also been noted to potentially reduce the pain and inflammation of arthritis. Turmeric contains an ingredient called curcumin, and there is anecdotal evidence that people who ingested diets high in curcumin appeared to have a lower risk of Alzheimer's disease. It is believed, based on recent data, that curcumin may be a natural inhibitor of the COX-2 enzyme. Although the evidence suggesting the COX-2 effects are all in experimental models, the proposed benefits of this herb would be consistent with what has been found in the lab. Whether turmeric is any better or safer for you than the standard pharmaceuticals is not clear, but this may be a reasonable thing to try if you are looking for a natural remedy. The usual dosage is 100 to 200 milligrams per day.

Boswellia

Boswellia, also know as Indian frankincense, comes from the bark of the boswellia serrata tree found in the hills of India. For hundreds of years, practitioners of traditional Indian medicine used it to reduce inflammation as well as pain and stiffness in joints. The active ingredient appears to be boswellian acid, which has been shown to have anti-inflammatory effects in animal models. Studies in humans do seem to support the potential anti-inflammatory and pain-relieving qualities of this herb in patients suffering from both rheumatoid arthritis and osteoarthritis.

The herb appears to be well tolerated by most people who take it in prescribed amounts, although some can experience diarrhea, nausea, bloating, and, rarely, rashes. All of these effects seem to disappear when medication is stopped. The length of time one should take the supplement is the source of some controversy; some claim that you should not take it for longer than eight to twelve weeks, although no long-term effects have been observed. If you are going to try boswellia, the typical dosage for arthritis is about 400 milligrams three times a day, which should be at least 60 percent boswellian acid, or about 240 milligrams per capsule. Because boswellia can potentially act as a blood thinner, check with your doctor if you are on any medications that might thin your blood before trying it.

Ginger

Chinese herbalists have used ginger for over two thousand years as a medication to help cure a wide variety of ailments, as well as a flavoring in a variety of foods. If you have been to any one of the thousands of sushi bars that have sprung up all over the United States and elsewhere, you no doubt have had the opportunity to taste ginger. You might have tasted it as a child when your mother gave you ginger ale to help settle an upset stomach. Ginger has been reported to have a number of medicinal uses, including a digestive aid, antinausea medication (even during pregnancy), common cold medication, and a pain reliever and anti-inflammatory. Ginger may work by decreasing the activity of some of the inflammatory prostaglandins, as well as improving blood flow to your joints by acting as a natural blood thinner. Studies have demonstrated that ginger can help reduce the pain and stiffness people have with arthritis.

Ginger comes in a number of different forms that, if taken according to appropriate dosing, can achieve a similar effect. You can take ginger root or powder, drink ginger tea, or take ginger in pill form. You can follow the dosing schedule on the following page to determine the appropriate amount of each preparation to take.

Ginger can occasionally lead to severe gastrointestinal distress with diarrhea and bloating, and can even stimulate an irregular heartbeat if taken in too high a dose. In addition, because ginger is a natural blood thinner, you need to be careful if you are taking any other medications that might thin your blood, or if you are prone toward bleeding.

At least two studies have shown that a combination of ginger, turmeric, and boswellia can offer significant relief from the pain and

Ginger extract in pills	100–200 mg/3 times a day
Fresh ginger root	$1/4$–$1/2$ inch peeled, sliced root/ 3 times a day
Fresh powdered ginger	$1/2$–1 teaspoon/3 times a day (it can be mixed with hot water)
Ginger tea	3–4 cups a day (the bag must be steeped for at least 5 min)

stiffness of both rheumatoid arthritis and osteoarthritis. Although direct comparisons between these remedies and traditional medications have not been done, each herb does seem to have some benefit, especially when combined. If you are looking for a more natural approach to treating your arthritis symptoms, turmeric, boswellia, and ginger might be a good choice for you.

Bromelain

Bromelain is a protein-digesting enzyme that is found in pineapples and has been known since the 1800s. It was found to be concentrated in the stems of pineapples and was formulated as a medicinal product beginning in the 1950s, although many native cultures used pineapple to treat a wide variety of ailments long before the discovery of bromelain. Bromelain is believed to reduce the amount of prostaglandins in a different fashion than NSAIDs and COX-2 inhibitors. Bromelain also appears to reduce the activity of fibrin, which is involved in the formation of blood clots and is also being studied as a potential blood thinner. Studies in animals and at least one study in humans seem to support that bromelain can reduce pain in patients with osteoarthritis. Adding other enzymes such as trypsin and rutin may increase the activity of the enzyme in arthritis.

Bromelain comes in capsule form. The appropriate dosage is not universally agreed to, but it ranges from 100 to 500 milligrams three times a day. If you are allergic or sensitive to pineapple you should not take bromelain, and if you have problems with bleeding or are on blood thinners bromelain is probably not the product for you. Numerous other potential benefits to bromelain are also being studied, including potential antitumor and antibacterial activities of the enzyme.

Cartilage and Collagen

Many products containing natural sources of cartilage and/or collagen have been touted as reducing inflammation and possibly repairing joint damage. Proponents of these products, which include such things as shark cartilage, chicken collagen, type II collagen (the type most commonly found in joint cartilage), and gelatin, just to name a few, believe that consuming natural forms of these constituents of cartilage can reduce inflammation and help to reconstitute injured cartilage. Unfortunately, the scientific basis for this does not appear to be solid. Human studies up to this time have been limited and the results have been mixed.

Of greater concern are the potential side effects of these products, which include nausea, vomiting, fatigue, allergic reaction (especially if you are allergic to the animal product from which the substance is derived), and even reports of hepatitis. There is even a theoretical concern that if the animals that the product is derived from were contaminated with mad cow disease, you could potentially be exposed, although no cases have been reported at this time, and with the epidemic in Europe apparently under control the risk is certainly extremely low. However, with so little data to support the benefits and with the potential for significant side effects, you should try these products only with great caution.

Numerous other herbal remedies have been reported to be the miracle savior for people with arthritis. Unfortunately, most of these rely on sketchy scientific research (or, worse yet, none at all) and depend on the reports of a small number of people who describe miraculous results. This is not to say that you may not gain some benefit from some of these compounds, but without studies to at least provide some reassurance of their safety and support the claims of benefits they might provide, you should use these remedies with some caution. If you are still not sure, talk to your doctor.

Acupuncture

Acupuncture has been around for more than three thousand years and has been used throughout Asia to treat a wide assortment of ailments, including pain and stiffness from arthritis, cancer, heart disease, bowel problems, and depression. Theories abound as to how acupuncture works. Many practitioners of acupuncture believe that your body has a life energy called *chi* that flows through your body through a series of *meridians*, or checkpoints. This life energy controls all of the organs in your body, and when your chi is blocked it makes you susceptible to illness, including arthritis. Acupuncture rebalances and unblocks the flow of energy and restores the body to its natural balance, allowing it to heal.

Others have theorized that acupuncture increases your body's natural pain relievers, called *endorphins*, therefore reducing the pain from your arthritis and other painful conditions. It may also work by relaxing muscle spasms and therefore decreasing pain around the joints, as well as inducing relaxation, which can lead to an overall feeling of well-being. Regardless of the reason, there is no question that many people with arthritis benefit from acupuncture.

Donald is a seventy-four-year-old retired accountant who has suffered from severe osteoarthritis of his hands, knees, and feet for several years. He used to be very active, golfing at least two times a week, taking regular walks on the beach with his wife, and building model airplanes. He had to give up all these activities because of the severity of his pain. He started an exercise program and lost twenty pounds, which gave him some relief, and tried numerous over-the-counter, prescription, and natural medications. He either had side effects from the medications or they simply didn't help.

Despite great pessimism and only on the insistence of his wife, Donald agreed to try acupuncture for up to eight sessions. For the first few times he went, he got relief, but it was not long lasting. However, after about the fifth or sixth treatment, he began noticing pain relief that would last for at least two to three days. As he continued to go, his pain and stiffness continued to improve, and now he is back to golfing and building model airplanes. He goes to the acupuncturist about every two to three weeks, or when his symptoms flare up.

Acupuncture is done by inserting extremely thin needles (about the width of two to four hairs) into the area that is in pain, or into other areas that may seem unrelated but are along the meridian that involves the part of the body causing the discomfort. Insertion of the needles is usually not painful when done by an experienced practitioner. The needles are then left in for several minutes before they are removed. Often people sense an almost immediate relaxation that lasts throughout the entire treatment session.

Several studies have now demonstrated that acupuncture reduces the pain and stiffness associated with osteoarthritis, as well as numerous other painful conditions, including fibromyalgia and chronic back pain. If you want to give acupuncture a try, you should start by going once or twice a week, and give it six to twelve sessions to see if it might help you. The amount of times you go will depend not only on your schedule, but on your wallet, as most insurance plans do not cover the cost of acupuncture. Over time, the benefits often begin to last longer, and you may be able to cut down on the frequency of visits to every two weeks or less.

It is important to find an acupuncturist who is experienced, and you should choose one in much the same way as you would choose your family doctor. Ask your family or friends if they know of anyone who might be good and experienced, or you can ask your personal physician as well.

Magnet Therapy

You have probably seen people walking around with magnets taped to a part of their body that is in pain. Magnet therapy has been around for a while, but has increased in popularity of late, with all types of magnetic braces, mattresses, and other devices now available for purchase. MRI scans use magnetic charges to create images of extremely high quality without any radiation exposure. Magnet therapy is based on the theory that the body is made of billions of magnetic charges and that when these charges are out of alignment or polarized toward either the positive or negative, cells do not function properly, leading to disease, including arthritis. By applying magnets to the areas of the body that are affected, you can realign the charges and alter nervous system impulses and blood flow. Increased oxygen is delivered to the tissues, and pain and inflammation in the joint are reduced. Some also believe that magnet therapy helps to dissolve calcium deposits in joints.

The scientific support for these theories is sketchy at best, although two small studies have implied that magnetic therapy may help to diminish pain. Most physicians, however, do not believe that magnets provide any medicinal benefit. Some products are quite expensive, while others cost only a few dollars, without any clearly discernible difference in the type of magnetic field they generate. So if you do choose to try magnet therapy in spite of the dearth of scientific proof of any real benefit, don't spend too much of your hard-earned money. If you have a pacemaker, magnets can alter the programming, so avoid using them.

Massage, Rolfing, and Feldencritz

Massage has been used over the years to reduce muscle spasms and increase feelings of relaxation and well-being. As has been discussed throughout the book, tight muscles contribute to the pain and stiffness of arthritis by restricting motion, and muscle stretching and strengthening is the cornerstone of any successful program to prevent and treat osteoarthritis. Although exercise is still the preferred method of reducing muscle spasms over the long term, massage can provide substantial short-term relief in symptoms. If you can reduce muscle spasms, you may move more freely and notice a reduction in pain. Massage is usually most effective after an acute injury, but can also alleviate chronic pain to the point that you can do exercises that will help you overcome the pain and stiffness of osteoarthritis.

Rolfing is an aggressive form of massage that attempts to restore the body's alignment through forceful manipulation of muscles. Rolfing repositions the body so that all parts are correctly aligned with gravity, allowing for less stress on joints and ligaments and increased freedom of motion. The technique can be uncomfortable, but patients who have obtained relief from pain swear by it.

Feldencritz was developed in the 1960s and has gained a great deal of popularity over the years. Feldencritz practitioners use techniques of massage and manipulation of various muscle groups to determine which motions cause pain. Then, through a variety of techniques, they train the body to automatically adjust so that it avoids and compensates for the motion that causes pain. The next time you move a certain way that causes pain, the body will accommodate and avoid the movement that caused the pain. Over time, you learn to move in ways that allow you to do your normal activities with greater ease. The process can take a great deal of time to see the benefits, but as part of a comprehensive program, it can provide significant relief of symptoms.

Manipulation and Other Manual Techniques

Chiropractors and osteopaths have used osseous manipulation for years to relieve pain from a variety of causes. The theory of osseous manipulation is that the spinal column is the control center for the nervous system. When the spinal column is "out of alignment," transmission of neurological signals is impaired, and pain, dysfunction, and disease ensue. Osseous manipulation realigns the column, restores balance, and improves function. Forceful and gentle manipulation, use of "stimulators," and therapy techniques are used.

Despite its widespread popularity, research into the benefits of manipulation is surprisingly sparse. You need to use caution in choosing a chiropractor and be certain of your diagnosis going in. If you have diseases such as osteoporosis, forceful manipulation can lead to new fractures. Choosing a good chiropractor who is experienced in treating osteoarthritis and incorporates an exercise program into your treatment plan can help you to reduce your pain and stiffness and allow you to go back to some of the activities you enjoy.

Homeopathy

Homeopathy was introduced by Dr. Samuel Hahnemann in the late 1700s, and is a natural approach that combines thousands of homeo-pathic medications. The theory states that a disease, regardless of the cause, affects not only the organ that is "sick," but the whole body. Treating the whole body offers a more durable and lasting cure. Patients are evaluated and are given the smallest dosage possible of a specially prepared combination of medications that are tailored to that patient's problems. These medications often are things that would actually cause the symptoms the patient is experiencing, but when given at ultra-small doses help to cure the problem and restore the body's "life energy." Many patients have turned to homeopathy when traditional therapies have failed.

If you are considering going the route of homeopathy, carefully choose a practitioner with significant medical experience. Some home-opaths were originally trained as M.D.s and have the more traditional background to complement their practice. The science behind the practice of homeopathy is not as sophisticated as that of traditional medication, so exercise caution.

We've now reviewed the alternative therapies available to you to alleviate symptoms of osteoarthritis. This chapter is not intended to be a complete list of all natural, homeopathic, and physical remedies theorized to prevent or treat arthritis, but a review of the main options being tried by patients throughout this country. Many of you may say, "What about this berry I heard about from my Aunt Maybelle that cured all of her symptoms?" Hope springs eternal. The magic remedy to prevent and cure osteoarthritis still seems to be lacking, although some natural treatments hold promise and may be able to provide you significant relief of symptoms. Unfortunately, the miracle pill that will take away your pain does not yet exist, and exercise and diet are still the key to overcoming this disease.

Your Personalized Arthritis Strategy

You're ready to go. You've decided that you now have the tools you need to get back to living an active life. You've seen your parents struggle through their older years with pain and are determined to do everything in your power to prevent that from happening to you. But what's the next step? How do you decide which exercises you need to do, or which medications you need to take?

When choosing which exercises and medications are right for you, you need to consider a number of factors, including your age, level of fitness, whether you already have osteoarthritis, and the severity of your disease. What is right for your friends, siblings, or coworkers may be very different from what is right for you. Your game plan for preventing or defeating the pain and stiffness of osteoarthritis must be tailored to your individual needs and goals. This chapter will help you to establish your personalized arthritis strategy so that you can overcome the obstacles that you face in your war against osteoarthritis.

Step 1: Set Your Goals

The first step in conquering osteoarthritis is to establish what you hope to achieve with your arthritis game plan. In order to have an effective strategy for beating this disease, you need to understand what you are trying to accomplish. For some of you, preventing the initial injury that leads to the development of osteoarthritis is the key. For others, simply being able to get out of the house and walk without assistance or pain is the goal. The strategies required by these two scenarios would obviously be very different.

Setting realistic goals can be a challenge. If you used to hike Mount Everest by day and run the marathon by night, it may be hard to get used to the fact that your body may not allow you to return to those types of vigorous activities if you have well-established arthritis. This is not to say that you may not be able to go hiking and running on a treadmill, but a joint that is already arthritic may not be able to perform to the same degree that a normal joint would, even if you follow every direction in this book perfectly. Although your long-term goal may be to bike the length of the Pacific Coast Highway, you should not expect to do that in three months after being a couch potato for fifteen years. Setting up both short- and long-term goals is critical in achieving success. It's been said that success breeds success—in other words, as you meet your short-term goals and begin to notice improvement in your symptoms, you feel better not only physically, but emotionally as well. When you succeed, you are more likely to push yourself to the next level. If you set your goals too high or for too short a period of time, you can get discouraged and give up.

You also need to make sure you do not set your goals too low. Often when you are in pain, you find it hard to believe that one day you may be able to have an active and pain-free life. If getting out of bed in the morning is a painful experience and you are unable to walk to the bathroom, then walking through the local shopping mall or taking a stroll on the beach may seem like a world away. Setting that as your long-term goal, with a short-term goal of being able to walk down the hallway with only a cane, may be a good place to start.

How do you know where to start? Many of you will spend weeks to months procrastinating. You will think, "I want to make sure I don't do too much or too little," and instead do nothing, hoping that inspiration will hit and you will magically know exactly what you want to do. Or you may anticipate 90 percent improvement in symptoms after two weeks and set unrealistic goals.

The most important thing you can do is just to *get started*. You may find once you start that you were unrealistic in what you had hoped to achieve early on, or that you set your standards too low. If so, simply modify your goals.

You may find it helpful to make a chart diagramming your short- and long-term goals, with checkpoints along the way to assess your progress and determine whether you need to modify the game plan (see the table on page 140).

Understanding and setting realistic, obtainable goals without getting overly frustrated if you don't succeed immediately is the first step toward an effective arthritis strategy.

Step 2: Make Time

You have set the plan in motion. You have committed to the program and laid out your short- and long-term goals. Unfortunately, you are still working twelve hours a day and have three kids at home who need (and deserve) your attention. That's to say nothing of the chores around the house that need to get done, the party you are planning for your parents' big wedding anniversary, and the week in Paris you promised your spouse last year. You would be only too happy to start the plan to achieve your goals, but you simply don't have the time.

We all have busy, stressful lives, but you need to remember that your health and well-being are worth a few minutes a day. Setting aside time to exercise and eat healthy not only is a good idea, it is essential to living a long, healthy, and pain-free life. You will find that if you feel better, you will suffer from less stress, complete your work more efficiently and more quickly, and enjoy your free time more.

Map out your daily schedule carefully and try to find even a few minutes a day for yourself. If it is only ten minutes to start, that's better than nothing. Make sure to keep that time firm in your calendar—

Time Frame	Goals/Achievements
Start date	Resume short hikes in local hills with friends
	Lose 20 pounds
2-week checkpoint	Able to do more than expected; increase walk to 15 minutes, 4 blocks
4-week checkpoint	Success with goal 1: tolerating 20-minute walk
	Start work toward goal 2: walk on beach 20 minutes
	Lost 6 pounds
8-week checkpoint	Pain with beach walk; extend date for goal by 2 weeks
	Lost 11 pounds
10-week reassessment	Able to walk 20 minutes on beach; move to next goal
14-week checkpoint	Walked in shopping mall with minimal pain
	Lost 15 pounds
4-month checkpoint	Take walk on local trail for 10 to 15 minutes
Long-term checkpoint (6 to 9 months)	Take 20-minute hike in local hills

otherwise, you will find something to fill the space. In addition, try not to set the time aside too late in the day, as fatigue may prevent you from doing what you need to do, and exercise at night can make it harder for you to go to sleep.

Step 3: Figure Out What to Incorporate into Your Strategy

You've laid out your short- and long-term goals and have found that magical twenty to thirty minutes a day to devote to your exercises, but how do you know where to start and which exercises to do? Is a traditional or alternative medication needed for you to accomplish what you have set out to do? The answers may not seem evident at first. The level of exercise may be very different for the twenty-year-old competitive runner without any history of injury compared to the sixty-year-old former jogger with arthritis in the hips and knees who wants to get back to fast-paced walking for relaxation and cardiovascular benefit. This chapter will help you determine which exercises make the most sense for you based on your individual goals and needs.

There are some general rules you can follow when deciding which exercises are appropriate for the activity you wish to participate in. The joints most commonly affected by osteoarthritis are the knees, hips, spine, hands, and feet. The wrists, elbows, and ankles are affected less commonly. Most types of exercise involve walking or running in some way or another, leading to stress and strain on the joints of the legs, so exercises for the knees and hips are essential for those who want to return to an active lifestyle. Obviously, if you are an author with arthritis of the hands and want to get back to your typing, then the hand and wrist exercises are probably the most essential.

There is no arthritis strategy that can prevent all injuries, especially if you do things to an extreme. Despite the fantastic conditioning levels of professional athletes, most will go on to develop osteoarthritis at some point in the future. Although studies have clearly demonstrated that regular levels of moderate exercise do not lead to increased risk of the development of osteoarthritis, extreme levels can often precede arthritic changes in the joints. Sporadic exercise, such as that done by weekend warriors, can also lead to problems as well.

Your level of fitness will obviously have a big influence on the program you choose. If you have been a couch potato for the past several years, you will have to start at a much lower level of exercise at the beginning, regardless of whether you have osteoarthritis. You don't want to push too hard with aggressive strengthening exercises at the outset, as you are much more injury prone at these early stages than when you are in better shape. You may progress very quickly once you get started, but be careful not to overdo it at first.

The presence or absence of osteoarthritis will also influence the strategies you incorporate. If you are exercising and losing weight simply to prevent arthritis from setting in, or if you are competitive athletically, you will want to add strengthening exercises earlier than someone who already has arthritis. If you already have arthritis, you will probably need to progress more slowly with any strategy.

Increased body weight makes any exercise program more difficult and puts additional strain on your muscles and joints, not to mention your heart and lungs. Incorporating a weight reduction program at the beginning of your game plan along with exercise is essential. In addition, healthy eating habits improve energy and promote fitness, so changing your eating choices can be as important as initiating a fitness program.

Pain is often the greatest limiting factor in exercise for people with arthritis. If pain has been a significant barrier to exercise in the past, taking pain relievers prior to activity can often allow you greater progress with less discomfort. If your pain is severe or is limiting you from advancing in your arthritis strategy, talk to your doctor about the medication that is right for you, or try one of the over-the-counter alternatives if your doctor approves it. By incorporating all of these strategies together, your chance to achieve success with your arthritis game plan will increase exponentially.

Step 4: Choose Exercises to Meet Your Goals

As has been discussed many times before, different activities require different muscle and joint groups. The exercises you choose in order to get into shape for certain activities will differ according to many factors. Following are some suggested exercises that might help you to prevent injury and the future development of osteoarthritis.

Walking and Jogging

Walking is still the most common form of exercise that people participate in. It is also the activity that most of us do throughout our whole lives, whether it is going from the bedroom to the kitchen, or walking around at the mall. Walking is also a wonderful form of aerobic exercise. Jogging, although aerobically an even better form of exercise, puts additional stress and strain on the knees and feet. Jogging is more likely to cause injury if you run on extremely hard surfaces or on uneven ground, as you are more likely to twist an ankle or knee. In fact, if you already have osteoarthritis of the knees, it is not recommended that you take up jogging, as the force that is constantly transmitted to your knees can aggravate your symptoms over time.

Before embarking on a walking or jogging program, it's important to remember a couple of tips. First, wear good shoes. Appropriate footwear is crucial to prevent injuries and ensure comfort. Good arch support and cushioned insoles are important, and it's equally important to be sized correctly. Investment in quality walking or running shoes can make all the difference in the world, and proper fitting is a vital part of that investment. Second, appropriate orthotics for your shoes and knee braces can help if you have foot problems or a previous history of knee injury.

Exercises to strengthen and stretch the quadriceps are essential if you have arthritis and are trying to get a walking program started or if you are a casual jogger and want to prevent injury. A program of at least five to ten minutes per day is critical in helping to avoid joint damage and can allow you to increase your activity level at a more rapid pace. Loosening up the muscles around the hip joint is also important and should be incorporated into any strategy you undertake. Foot, ankle, and back exercises (depending on your history of problems in these areas) can be considered as well. If you already have existing arthritis and need to get back to walking, taking acetaminophen or an anti-inflammatory about thirty minutes prior to walking can help.

Joggers need to be even more cautious than runners, as they are at greater risk for twisting a knee or ankle and put greater force on their feet and knees than walkers. Microdamage to the cartilage can occur and start the process of osteoarthritis. If you begin to notice pain after you run, you may need to either cut back or take a break. Pain often causes you to use improper form, putting not only the injured joint at risk, but other joints as well.

Marathon and other distance runners are at greater risk for injury. The constant pounding on the knees, hips, and feet can lead to micro-damage to the cartilage and the eventual development of arthritis. If you are going to undertake this type of strenuous running program, you need to watch your diet very closely, as you can be in danger of losing muscle mass and too much weight if you don't ensure adequate protein and caloric intake. A vigorous regimen of loosening up is cru-cial. Never push yourself if you are beginning to notice pain or stiff-ness in your muscles or joints. Unfortunately, almost any sport greatly increases the risk of developing future problems when taken to extremes. Remember, your body was not constructed to run twenty-six miles in three hours. You need to spend months, even years, prepar-ing for such a grueling run. If you try to do this without a proper training regimen, your risk of injury increases greatly.

Hiking

Think of hiking as walking on uneven ground. Therefore, all the guide-lines for walking we just discussed apply, along with a few other tips specific to hiking. Most hikers carry a backpack of some sort. Do not overload it, as this will put increased stress and strain on your back, which can cause you to become off balance, leading to falls or back, knee, and ankle strains.

Make sure you are in good shape before going out. You may feel that you could walk a couple of miles easily, but that is very different from hiking a couple of miles on hills, carrying a backpack, on uneven or mountainous terrain. Once you have started down the trail, you may not be able to turn back—and injuries tend to occur when you are tired, so be careful. Wear sturdy shoes and, if you have arthritis in your knees, appropriate bracing.

Golf

Golf has become an increasingly popular sport, although it may not be the best source of aerobic fitness. Golf courses are often about four miles long, certainly a reasonable distance to walk for aerobic fitness; however, many golfers ride a cart around the links, leaving little cardiovascular benefit to the exercise. Although I am not recommending that you walk the course and lug around your twenty-five-pound golf bag, you can walk with a handcart to pull your bag, or use a caddie. Walking the course is certainly the preferred option from a health perspective.

The most common areas of injury for golfers are, in order, the lower back, shoulders, and wrists. In fact, some estimates state that up to 80 percent of regular golfers will develop osteoarthritis. Golf used to be viewed as a recreational sport, and fitness and golf were not thought to be related. On the professional level, golfers are now taking fitness much more seriously, especially since Tiger Woods started tearing up the courses. Although improved club technology has contributed to farther drives and better shotmaking, the increased emphasis on exercise has probably had an equally significant impact.

Golfers, depending on form and fitness, use almost all of their muscle groups throughout the swing. Strength is less important than flexibility, as a fluid swing with all muscle groups acting in unison is essential for a long and straight shot. This is not to say that strengthening exercises should be ignored. An appropriate muscle strengthening program, especially for the shoulder girdle to prevent rotator cuff injuries, should be incorporated into any golf fitness program.

Proper swing mechanics can go a long way toward prevention of injury. A herky-jerky or disjointed swipe at the ball can lead to muscle strain, most commonly in the middle and lower back but in the arms and legs as well. If you notice that you are prone to muscular aches and pains on a consistent basis after a round of golf, you may have a problem with your swing mechanics. Spending a session or two with a club professional may be enough to diagnose the problem and get you straightened out.

If your swing mechanics are not the problem, then a general stretching program is an absolute necessity. Focusing on particular areas, such as the lower back and shoulders, is essential, and many golfers not only do these exercises at home, but do modified versions of them while on the course. If you notice some slight stiffness midway through a round, stopping for a couple of minutes to do some of your stretches can help you avoid muscle strain and injury, especially if you have arthritis in the joint around the affected area. However, if the pain or stiffness is anything more than mild, continuing to play can lead to further injury; you should probably not finish the round.

Whether you already have osteoarthritis or are trying to avoid it, some regular exercises can help you maintain golf fitness. These include a general program of stretches focusing on the lower back, shoulders, wrists, and knees. If you already have arthritis in a particular joint, obviously your program should address that area in one way or another. Start doing daily stretching for ten to fifteen minutes, regardless of whether you are playing that day, using the exercises described in "The First Quarter." Over time, complementing these with some of the strengthening exercises, especially for the back and shoulders, can be considered. On top of that, do additional stretches on the course prior to taking any practice swings and, depending on symptoms, a couple of times throughout the round. These usually involve the lower back, as well as any area you have had problems with in the past, and should take one to two minutes at most.

In fact, you can use your clubs to help enhance some of the stretches described in "The First Quarter" to increase the range of some of the twists. Some specific exercises that you may find helpful prior to getting on the course and throughout the round include the following.

1. **Overhead Stretch.** Hold your driver above your head with your arms straight. Slowly lean to one side, keeping your arms and head straight. Repeat, leaning to the other side. Repeat cycle five times. You can also twist at the waist.

2. **Behind-the-Back Twist.** Hold your driver behind you with your arms straight down. Slowly twist at the waist from one side to the other. Repeat five times.

3. **Forward Flexion.** Hold your driver in front of you. With your legs straight, lean over and try to touch the ground. Get up slowly. Repeat five to ten times.

Obviously, you can't lie on the ground while on the course, which is required by many of the exercises described in "The First Quarter." But doing small things to keep loose on the course can help to reduce pain and the risk of injury.

Maintaining a healthy weight is also essential to golf fitness. As you look around the professional golfing circuit these days, you no longer see golfers with large bellies, because back problems were becoming rampant. Ideal body weight not only prevents injuries and helps prevent the development of osteoarthritis, but is important for other reasons as well. The heavier you are, the more likely you are to fatigue when you are out on the course for five hours. Fatigue causes you to lose proper swing mechanics and makes injury more likely.

Finally, if it is true that up to 80 percent of golfers may at some point develop osteoarthritis, then you may already have pain when you step out on the course. If you are already taking acetaminophen or other pain relievers as needed, consider taking a dose about thirty minutes before teeing off. You may find that your round is a lot more enjoyable with a lot less pain.

Tennis

Tennis can be a wonderful form of exercise that benefits your aerobic health and your joints. However, it can put a great deal of strain on your hips, knees, back, shoulders, and, of course, the elbow and forearm (the cause of so-called tennis elbow). The quick side-to-side and forward-backward motions can lead to injury, including muscle and ligament strains and microtrauma to the cartilage of the knees and hips. The overhead serve can be particularly problematic if you are already suffering from shoulder or rotator cuff damage. With newer composite rackets, the vibrations are slightly less than those of the older aluminum varieties, though the firm grip and turning of the forearm can continue to lead to stress and strain around the forearm and elbow, resulting in tennis elbow.

Tennis elbow, as it is commonly known, in medical terms is called *lateral epicondylitis*. Several tendons attach along a bony structure known as the *lateral epicondyle*, and it is these tendons and the muscles associated with them in the forearm that are involved with tennis elbow. When these muscles and tendons get inflamed, irritated, or torn, you can develop pain around the elbow and into the forearm. Although tennis elbow is not commonly associated with the development of arthritis, it can prevent you from playing or alter your swing mechanics, leading to injuries of the shoulders, wrists, or hands.

You can help to prevent tennis elbow by strengthening your hands, wrists, and elbows, as the muscles that travel through the forearm are responsible for many of the movements of the wrists and hands. Other than the routine listed in "The First Quarter," here are a couple of other exercises you may find useful.

1. **Rubber Band Finger Extension.** With your elbow bent at your side, take a rubber band and place it around the base of your thumb and your other fingers. Spread your fingers apart as far as you can and hold for three to five seconds and relax. Repeat five to ten times on each hand. Do this exercise one to two times a day. As you get stronger, you can use a thicker rubber band or place it closer to your fingertips.

2. **Rubber Ball Squeeze.** Hold a soft ball in your hand and squeeze it as tightly as you can for three to five seconds. Repeat ten times on each hand once or twice a day.

3. **Desk Wrist Extension and Flexion.** Place your forearm on a table or desk with your wrist and hand over the edge. While contracting the muscles in your forearm and making a fist, move your hand up and down ten times. Repeat with the other hand. You can add a one- to two-pound weight or can of food to increase the intensity of the exercise. Repeat this exercise with your palm up and down.

If you already have tennis elbow, rest and ice is the best short-term treatment. Occasionally, it will not resolve on its own and you will need to see a doctor or therapist for further treatment, which can include anti-inflammatory medications, physical therapy, a cortisone injection, bracing, and, rarely, surgery. You may find that a change in racket or a session or two with a professional trainer may help you to correct your mechanics and help to reduce the tension and strain on the fore-arm and elbow.

The shoulder can be of particular concern, especially if you have a powerful overhead serve. The serve can put a great deal of stress and strain on the shoulder joint itself, the capsule surrounding it, and the muscles and tendons of the rotator cuff and upper shoulder. In addition, if you already have arthritis of the neck or shoulder, trying to get full extension during the serve can lead to a great deal of pain. An aggressive stretching and strengthening program around the shoulder is essential in preventing injury and will allow for the most effective serve. Using the exercises in "The First Quarter" can go a long way toward helping to prevent injury.

You must maintain proper form, as an awkward serve can lead to strains and tears of muscles, tendons, and the joint capsule. If you already are noticing pain in the shoulder joint, then an overhead serve may not be the best idea. Drop down to the side for a while, as this puts much less strain on your shoulder joint and rotator cuff. If the pain persists after you have given it some time off, you may need to see a doctor. Also, if you have problems in the neck and shoulder region, avoiding the overhead serve altogether may be a good idea.

The knees and hips are also at significant risk with tennis. It is clear from medical literature that sudden movement is much more likely to cause injury and cartilage damage than is continuous, fluid motion. Tennis requires constant stopping and starting, and keeping the muscles and joints of the legs loose and in good shape is crucial to prevent damage. It's important to stretch each day and to warm up at least ten to fifteen minutes before you play. In addition, walking, swimming, and biking will help to increase lower-extremity strength and overall fitness as well.

If you have osteoarthritis in your hips or knees, you may find that a competitive game may be too much at first. Working yourself back into shape and stretching every time you step on the court is absolutely necessary. Even hitting the ball for thirty minutes can be a good form of exercise. Eventually, if you are diligent with your fitness regimen, you may find that you are able to get back to a more competitive game.

James is a seventy-three-year-old retired advertising executive who played tennis in college but suffered torn cartilage in his left knee about twenty years ago. He underwent surgery and did well until about three years ago, when he tried to start playing "competitive" tennis at the club. After about an hour on the court, his knee would swell up and begin to hurt. He stopped playing. Soon James began experiencing pain when he walked up a flight of stairs or got in and out of a car. He was quite frustrated because he had envisioned getting back out on the tennis court at least two to three days a week once he was retired.

He went to his doctor, who did an x-ray and told him he had osteoarthritis in his left knee and advised him to take some acetaminophen. James asked about playing tennis, but his doctor didn't say much. He decided to embark on an aggressive exercise program like that outlined in "The First Quarter": swimming fifteen minutes a day, walking every other day, and stretching and strengthening exercises for his knees, hips, back, and shoulders. He often took acetaminophen prior to his workout if he noticed some discomfort. Over two months, his knee pain diminished by over 50 percent and he began doing some volleying on the court. Although he has not entered the over-seventy tournament at the club quite yet, he is starting to play some short twenty- to thirty-minute sets.

Through an aggressive program, you can get back to playing tennis, even if you already have osteoarthritis.

Basketball

Reading this section won't turn you into the next Shaquille O'Neal or Michael Jordan, but these athletes are two of the best examples of what constant pounding on the court can do to your legs. At the tender age of twenty-nine, Shaq was already afflicted with osteoarthritis in his toe, which held him out of a portion of the 2001–2002 season and may require him to have further surgery. (He has already been under the knife once for this problem.) Michael Jordan, still quite young at thirty-nine, underwent arthroscopic surgery on his knee because of pain and was found to have "normal wear and tear as would be expected for someone who has been through what he has."

The constant pounding on the hips, knees, ankles, and feet that basketball entails can lead to significant problems if you don't take care of yourself. Basketball, like tennis, requires quick cuts, side-to-side motions, and frequent changes in direction. The most common basketball injury is the ankle sprain, which is why you see the majority of college and professional basketball players wearing high-tops: they protect against the turning in of the ankles that can lead to ankle sprains. However, by using high-tops, you may be putting your knee at greater risk. All-time NBA leading scorer Kareem Abdul-Jabbar never wore high-tops during his twenty-one-year career and has no evidence of any arthritis in his knees. He attributes this to excellent conditioning throughout his career and to never wearing high-tops (he still works out aggressively and is in fantastic shape). He feels that preventing the ankle from turning leads to increased stress and strain on the knees, and eventually to damage.

The ankles are certainly an area of concern in basketball, and any comprehensive basketball conditioning program should include stretching and strengthening around the ankles. However, the ankle, no matter how many times you sprain it, is relatively exempt from the development of osteoarthritis. The knees, hips, and feet are at much greater risk. Appropriate footwear is essential in absorbing some of the shock that comes from the jumping and running of basketball. If you have a history of ankle sprains, then you may need high-tops, but if you have had knee problems in the past, high-tops may not be ideal. A protective knee brace can help. Elastic bandages can give you some mild support and will possibly help if you don't have a previous history of knee problems, but if your knee is already arthritic you may need to have a special brace made to better protect you. These braces are covered by most insurance plans, including Medicare, so see your doctor if you think you need one.

Preventing the problem before it occurs is obviously the first choice. An exercise program that involves stretching of the lower back, hips, knees, ankles, and feet before every game is an absolute necessity.

Increasing quadriceps strength can go a long way toward averting knee arthritis in the future, as well as maintaining flexibility for the quick changes in direction that basketball requires. In addition, the stronger your legs are, the better your shot is likely to be. You will get more elevation on your jump shot and increase your shooting range.

Basketball, like tennis, requires a great deal of physical stamina. You are definitely more prone toward injury when you are tired, so sustaining a good aerobic fitness program is crucial, especially if you are a weekend warrior who plays only occasionally. If you tire easily, you will tend to move awkwardly, which makes you more likely to twist a knee or ankle. Always remember, preventing that first injury and damage to your cartilage is the most important thing you can do to prevent or slow the development of osteoarthritis.

If you have arthritis, basketball may become a much more difficult sport to participate in. Playing full court may be more than your joints or level of fitness can handle. An aggressive stretching and strengthening program may help you to get back to being able to play, as will using appropriate footwear and orthotics if you already have pain in the feet. However, you may find that despite all of this, two hours of full court basketball is a bit too much for those achy knees and feet. Switching to a half-court game, or playing with a large enough group that you can substitute in and out as needed to give yourself a break, can be helpful. You should not push your body to the point of exhaustion, but instead work in short spurts; this should allow you recovery time and result in your being able to do more. If you play in ten- to fifteen-minute increments and then give yourself a five- to ten-minute rest, you may find that you are able to play longer and more effectively, and with less pain. Whether or not you have osteoarthritis, you can play basketball if you are willing to work at it.

Softball and Baseball

You would think that the weekend softball game you play with your friends wouldn't be a source of pain. However, when you take a big swing and miss and feel that pull in your back, or when you try to stop suddenly as you go into second base and you get that sharp pain in your knee, you realize that these supposedly noncontact sports can lead to significant injury. You read in the papers all the time about baseball players getting injured—and these are well-conditioned athletes! (At least most of them are.)

You will notice that before every organized baseball game the players loosen up for about fifteen minutes. Baseball and softball players spend much of their time standing or sitting, and then suddenly spring into action to run after a fly ball or take their turn at bat. These sudden motions can lead to joint, muscle, and ligament damage, because the muscles and ligaments have tightened up while the player was inactive.

Stretching exercises are the key to preventing joint problems while playing baseball and softball. The most common areas of injury include the back, knees, and ankles (except for pitchers, who most often suffer injuries to the shoulders and elbows). Although some of today's power hitters, like Sammy Sosa, look as if they have spent all day at the gym lifting weights, bat speed is much more important. Before coming to the plate, especially if you have been on the bench for a while, a two-minute exercise regimen to loosen up the neck, shoulders, and back can help to prevent pulls and strains. These could include the stretching exercises in "The First Quarter," including but not limited to chair lower-back flexion (page 21), wall lunge (page 22), neck rotation (page 31), chin-to-collarbone stretch (page 32), neck extension (page 32), shoulder shrug (page 35), arm crossover (page 37), single shoulder grab (page 37), double shoulder grab (page 37), and elbow grab (page 38).

When playing the field, you need to keep moving to prevent yourself from stiffening up. Although you probably can't stand out there doing formal exercise, moving from side to side and shifting your weight from one foot to the other will help keep you loose. Appropriate footwear that gives you good traction without allowing your feet to get caught in the ground can help.

Baseball (and fast-pitch softball) pitchers obviously need to be concerned about the shoulder and elbow areas. In fact, pitchers under the age of twelve are told not to throw certain pitches because of the enormous stress and strain it puts on the elbow joint and the surrounding tendons and ligaments. One study revealed that approximately 40 percent of nine- to twelve-year-old pitchers suffered some sort of injury, and the elbow is particularly vulnerable during the active growth phase of adolescence (from ten to about sixteen). Rotator cuff and shoulder joint problems can occur due to overuse, improper pitching mechanics, or preexisting abnormalities within the joint and surrounding structures.

In children and adults, limiting the number of pitches thrown in a game and giving adequate rest between games pitched is essential. Stretching and strengthening exercises for the shoulder and elbow are an absolute necessity as well. Proper mechanics, including the arm follow-through and planting of the legs, can help you to reduce the risk of injury and subsequent cartilage damage. A daily workout regimen should focus on general stretching and strengthening exercises as well as overall aerobic fitness, as softball and baseball do not provide a significant aerobic workout.

If you have arthritis in the shoulders, elbows, or hands, your dream of becoming a major league pitcher may be dashed, although you can still probably play softball. Doing exercises focusing on your particular joints that are already arthritic and avoiding sudden movements as much as possible can help you to continue playing with minimal pain and discomfort.

Soccer

Soccer is one of the world's most aerobically demanding and popular sports. It can put a great deal of strain on your knees, hips, ankles, and feet, and injuries are quite common.

Soccer requires that you maintain a high level of aerobic fitness, so make sure that you are in good shape before you start playing. If you are significantly overweight or not at a top level of fitness, you should think twice before getting out on the field, as your risk of injury is increased. Stretching and strengthening the hips, knees, and ankles are crucial to preventing joint damage, and appropriate bracing for those with mild arthritis or a history of chronic ankle sprains can help prevent further problems. Appropriate footwear is a necessity, no matter what your age. If you already have moderate to severe arthritis, you may want to consider playing a different sport, as soccer may be too demanding.

Skiing (and Snowboarding)

There is a reason that some of the best orthopedic surgeons in the world are found not only at the major teaching hospitals, but in popular ski towns as well. Skiers are among the most injury-prone athletes, breaking bones of all varieties and tearing anterior cruciate ligaments and knee cartilage. The reasons skiers and snowboarders are prone to injury are several. Skiing is a recreational sport for most, with skiers taking an occasional weekend or week during the year to ski, rather than skiing regularly. The speeds and constant turns and changes of direction place stress on joints, ligaments, and muscles, and falls are quite common.

Getting into shape for that week in Aspen requires a significant commitment on your part. It is usually recommended that you start your ski fitness program six to eight weeks before you hit the slopes. The program needs to address strength, flexibility, and aerobic exercise. Although weight training to strengthen the lower-extremity muscles can certainly benefit skiers, an effective workout program can be done without weights as well. You should commit at least three days a week up to forty-five minutes a day to getting ready for your ski outing.

Jena and Janet are twenty-year-old college students who decided to spend their winter vacation together skiing. Although both work out minimally during the year, neither is in "good shape." Jena began an aggressive workout program that included flexibility and strengthening exercises for twenty-five minutes three times a week and riding the stationary bike for twenty to thirty minutes four times a week. Janet, on the other hand, did little to prepare for their trip except to buy the latest in ski fashions.

On the second day of the trip, Janet took a nasty fall when she lost control going too fast down a straightaway and tore two ligaments in her knee. She had to come back home and have surgery a week later. The doctors have told her that she will likely develop arthritis in that knee in about twenty to thirty years.

Jena finished the trip a little sore but was able to get down the black diamond hills by the end of the week and has already put down a deposit to go again during spring break.

Other than broken bones due to falls, most injuries that occur while skiing involve the knees, hips, and lower back. Focusing stretching and strengthening exercises in the muscle groups around those areas, as well as increasing abdominal muscle strength, can go a long way toward preventing injury. In addition to the exercises discussed in "The First Quarter," more advanced strengthening exercises can help you to prevent injury. These include the following:

1. **Stair Lunge.** Stand up straight with your legs spread out about shoulder-width apart. Step forward onto a stair, bending the front leg at the knee but not letting the knee extend in front of the toes. Try to keep the back leg straight, if possible, and bring the leg back down. Repeat ten times for each leg. If this is too hard, do it on a flat surface. This is a wonderful exercise to strengthen the quadriceps muscle.

2. **Standing Waddle.** Standing up, but in a slightly squatting position, and with your knees over or behind your toes, lift up on the balls of your feet and move your heels out. Do the same thing while bringing your legs back in. Repeat three more times.

3. **Lying Hip Abduction.** Lie on your side with your head resting comfortably on your hand or arm. Bend your lower leg and straighten your upper leg. Slowly lift your upper leg about two to three inches, then slowly lower it back down. Repeat ten times, then ten times on the other side. Do the same thing with your lower leg straight out and your upper leg crossed over it and the foot resting on the floor to start. Again, lift the upper leg about two to three inches off the floor while keeping it in front of you. Try to do this ten times, although that may be difficult at first.

4. **Kneeling Leg Curl.** Kneel down with your forearms resting on the floor and lift one leg up slowly and lower it back to the ground. Repeat with the other leg. The leg can stay bent or

straight, whatever is easier for you. Do six to ten repetitions on each leg.

5. **Hip Extension.** Kneel down with your forearms resting on the floor. Straighten one leg out and maintain your balance while keeping your back straight and looking at the floor. Bend the leg at the knee, bringing your foot up toward your head. Repeat up to ten times, then ten times with the other leg. This may be difficult if you are not in good shape, so don't hurt yourself trying it if you are not ready.

6. **Bending Foot Grab.** Lie down on your back on the floor with your knees bent and your feet flat on the ground. Place one hand under your head and the other arm straight at your side. Bend at the waist and try to touch your foot. Move slowly up and down. Repeat on the other side. Do ten repetitions on each side.

If you are in really good shape, try the following exercises. However, if you have any neck or back pain, you should avoid them.

1. **Lumbar Lift.** Lie flat on your back with your arms at your sides and your palms flat. Place your legs straight up in the air and hold them steady (you can cross your legs if it helps). Lift your buttocks and lower back off the floor gently. Repeat five to ten times.

2. **Lying Foot Grab.** Lie flat on your back with your arms straight out above your head. Lift one leg up and try to bring your hands up to touch your foot. Repeat with the other leg. Try to do five to ten repetitions per leg.

In addition to flexibility and strength, aerobic fitness is essential. Often, skiers and snowboarders will hit the slopes for six to ten hours in a given day. Most skiing injuries occur in the afternoon as fatigue sets in.

Skiing usually involves aggressive exercise for five- to seven-minute stretches, followed by a several-minute break as you get back on the lift and ride back up to the top. Aerobic programs that mimic this style can sometimes help you to get an edge. Some recommend that during your aerobic training you actually do bursts of activity followed by relatively relaxed cool-down periods over several cycles. For example, if you walk the treadmill as your form of aerobic exercise, you may go relatively slow with minimal incline for about five minutes to warm up, then increase speed and incline greatly for about seven minutes. After that, you may slow down again for about five minutes and then increase again, repeating this cycle three to four times. Others believe that simply getting in the best aerobic shape possible is the best way to prepare for the slopes.

Aerobic exercises that also increase lower-body strength and flexibility are probably ideal. The most logical choice for you may be a cross-country ski machine, which can simulate many of the movements involved in skiing and provides a good aerobic workout. However, unless you belong to a health club that has one, this may not be feasible. Stairclimbing, which is wonderful for the muscles of the thighs and calves but can be stressful for arthritic knees, is an excellent alternative. You don't necessarily need a stairclimbing machine to do this, as it can be done anywhere there is a flight of stairs that you can safely go up and down without a lot of traffic. If you vary the speed and direction, this can be an excellent workout alternative.

Appropriate gear is critical in preventing injuries as well. Boots that are well fitted and provide good ankle support can help decrease the risk of ankle fractures. Many more aggressive skiers and snowboarders, especially those who do moguls, wear knee braces even if they have never had a previous injury. If you have a previous history of injury or arthritis, you need to be even more cautious about getting into shape and using appropriate equipment and bracing. If your arthritis is at all advanced, you may want to consider a different sport.

Getting an early start in preparing for the ski season is vital. Unlike many other sports, where you can start at a leisurely pace and then work yourself into shape, when you ski you careen down a mountainside and are frequently forced to stop or change directions quickly. Even if you stay on the low intermediate hills, you can still reach speeds of up to forty miles per hour, more than enough to cause major injury if you turn or fall wrong. Because many skiers don't prepare in the off-season, skiing and snowboarding offer a relatively high risk of injury. You can enjoy skiing for many years with greater ease if you take the time to get yourself ready with an appropriate exercise program.

Football

No medical expert would recommend tackle football as a logical form of exercise. The average professional football player's career is only four years, mostly because of the wide variety of injuries that occur—and this does not account for the numerous players in high school and college who suffer severe damage to their bones, joints, and ligaments from a multitude of problems, despite a strong emphasis on fitness and improvements in protective gear. *Sports Illustrated* just reported the high cost that professional football players pay for participating in the game, with osteoarthritis being the number one problem. The reasons for this are abundantly clear if you have ever been tackled trying to run or catch a football.

Although being in the best possible physical shape will help you to some degree, there is no way to prevent football-related injuries. Maintaining an ideal weight can help as well, as can making sure not to mask injuries with pain medications, which can result in further joint damage. The best possible advice is not to play if you already have arthritis, and understand the risks if you don't.

If you want to play a friendly game of touch football on your lawn or in the park, that is a different story. The knees and ankles are the most prone to injury, and stretching and strengthening around these areas can help you to enjoy the game more. If you are playing quarterback, make sure to loosen up the shoulders and neck prior to playing; no matter what position you're playing, do ten to fifteen minutes of general flexibility exercises prior to playing, focusing on the lower back, hips, knees, and ankles. Proper footwear, especially if the ground is wet and muddy, can help prevent you from twisting your knees and ankles.

Volleyball

Volleyball has become an increasingly popular sport in gyms and on beaches around the United States. Approximately 800 million people in 130 countries presently play. Almost all joint and muscle groups are involved in the various maneuvers required in volleyball, which include serving, setting, jumping, diving, spiking, and blocking. Most injuries you get playing volleyball are relatively minor, but can lead to future problems if not addressed properly.

Most injuries in volleyball are related to jumping and spiking. If you land awkwardly, ankle sprains occur when your ankle turns inward (such as when landing on the ground or on someone's foot). Occasionally knee injuries can occur as well, which include sprains and, less commonly, cartilage or ligament tears. Strains of the neck, shoulders, and lower back can arise as well.

Hand and finger injuries crop up frequently, with so-called jammed fingers seen most commonly. If you have played volleyball with any regularity, you have certainly jammed your finger at least once. Usually it heals on its own. A jammed finger is really a sprain (tear) of the ligaments that run on the sides of your joints (the collateral ligaments). If you jam your finger, stop playing until the finger heals and tape the finger to the one next to it. This forms a natural splint and allows the finger to heal properly. Usually you can return to playing within a few weeks; however, if you try to return too soon, you can reinjure the ligament and eventually cause joint damage. Rarely you can break a finger playing, so if you don't seem to be healing properly, or if the injured finger becomes very black-and-blue, you should see your doctor and get an x-ray.

A flexibility program focusing on the areas of potential injury can help you to play longer and free of symptoms. You should spend fifteen minutes before every match or practice on a variety of stretches for your shoulders, fingers, back, knees, and ankles. In addition, stretching and strengthening these areas at least three times a week can help you to prevent injuries in the future. Your jumping technique may put you at increased risk of injury, especially if you land very close to the net (the center line). By jumping straight up and down, you may be able to avoid landing awkwardly and twisting your knees or ankles.

If you have a minor strain or sprain, listen to your body and take a few days off. If you develop pain in your lower back, knee, or shoulder, a short course of an anti-inflammatory medication may help you to get back to playing more quickly. If you notice pain after playing, switching to a softer court can help alleviate muscle and joint strains and reduce the wear and tear you experience with the frequent jumping volleyball requires. Even if you already have osteoarthritis, an appropriate flexibility and strengthening program can allow you to play and enjoy volleyball for many years to come.

Bicycling

There are several ways to enjoy bicycling—stationary biking, recumbent bikes, riding on the beach, and advanced mountain biking, just to name a few. The stress that each type puts on your body can vary greatly, although all can be fantastic methods of building aerobic fitness. Bicycling is a great way to strengthen your leg muscles. Some of you who have knee arthritis may find riding the bicycle painful—especially mountain biking, as the additional pounding can take its toll.

The knees are by far the joints most commonly affected by bicycling, although those with back problems may develop increased pain because of lack of lumbar support. Using a recumbent bicycle usually alleviates the discomfort. You may want to embark on a quadriceps and hamstring flexibility and strengthening program prior to starting to bike. Start gradually, as often you don't feel the discomfort of biking until after you have completed it. And don't start out with those bumpy mountain trails. Flat terrain or stationary bikes cause less pounding and may be easier for your joints to tolerate at first. You will, over time, gain endurance, strength, and confidence, which will allow you to progress to those more difficult mountain trails.

Appropriate equipment is essential, especially if you are going mountain biking. Wear a helmet at all times, as well as protective pads for your elbows and knees. (Those riding the stationary bikes can obviously ignore this advice.) Purchase a bike that is appropriate for the type of riding you are going to do and is the appropriate size. Make sure the seat is adjusted to the correct height as well.

In-Line Skating

What was once reserved for youngsters on California beaches now has caught on with adults, and in-line skaters can be seen in almost every neighborhood across America. Injuries like those seen in skiers, including broken bones and torn knee ligaments, are also seen commonly in in-line skaters—especially adults, who may not be as experienced, but want to try to keep up with their children.

If you want to start skating, you should follow a few basic rules.

1. Make sure you are in good shape. In-line skating is a wonderful form of aerobic exercise, but requires you to maintain a high level of fitness. You may want to start an aerobic fitness program for four to six weeks before you take up this sport. When you do start, don't go too far, because you may find yourself tiring out quicker than you expect, and you could have a long way to travel back to where you started. Injuries occur more often when you are fatigued.
2. Wear protective gear, including a helmet, kneepads, and elbow-pads, and be certain that your skates fit correctly and are comfortable.
3. Loosen up your legs prior to skating.
4. Start a knee and hip strengthening program at least three times a week, preferably for four to six weeks before starting.
5. If you already have osteoarthritis in your knees, you need to be especially careful when you go skating. You should consider wearing a brace, even if your knee isn't giving you any problems.

With careful preparation and planning, you can get into better shape and avoid major injury.

Aerobics

Aerobics became very popular in the 1980s as millions of people started taking classes where they jumped and danced and moved to music together. An instructor would run the class with upbeat music and you would follow along for up to an hour, usually working up quite a sweat. Numerous new forms of aerobic exercise sprang from aerobics, including dancercise, jazzercise, and every other -cise you can think of. You no longer have to join a gym to do aerobics, as your local video store may have a hundred tapes of varying levels and types of workouts for you to choose from. Many of you may have tried aerobics classes but found that your legs and knees would constantly ache after workouts, and gave it up within a few weeks of starting.

How do you know whether aerobics is right for you, and which type makes the most sense? Aerobics is a wonderful way to improve cardiovascular fitness and increase muscle and joint flexibility as well. The difficulty comes with the jumping, which can lead to increased pain and swelling if you have a knee problem. The constant pounding as you hop on one leg, run in place, or get up and down off the floor several times can trigger pain in the legs and back.

Determining your level of fitness is the first step. Remember that when you are fatigued, you are more prone to injury. Do not start with a class that is too difficult. You can always move to a more challenging class if you find the one you start with too easy. Most gyms will stratify groups from beginners to advanced. Most classes run close to an hour, but if you are not aerobically fit, you may be able to do only the first fifteen or twenty minutes. You can slowly increase by three to five minutes a week as your fitness level improves. If you push too hard for too long, you are more likely to make a mistake and hurt yourself. Preventing the first injury is still the best way to prevent arthritis.

Because aerobics can be high-impact exercises, you need to be very careful if you have arthritis. The pounding may be too much for your joints to take, so a low-impact class would probably suit you better. Some of you may find that even that is too much, and you may need to start a home stretching and strengthening program before you even consider an aerobics class. Most aerobic classes work on improving flexibility, but you still may want to loosen up a little bit before you start.

You can often choose classes based on the types of music you like, or based on a particular type of dance. Have fun! If you enjoy the exercise you are doing, you are much more likely to stick with it. Take a class with a friend, or use it as an opportunity to meet new people. Just make sure to listen to your body and not push yourself too far.

Swimming

As you read in "The First Quarter," warm water exercises can help you to overcome the pain and stiffness of osteoarthritis. What if you want to get back to swimming laps or in the ocean or lake? Is the routine any different for you?

A couple of simple rules will help you to get back into swim shape. As you already know, swimming is one of the best forms of aerobic exercise, and puts much less stress and strain on your joints than many other sports. Although warm water is necessary for an aquatic exercise program, you may not want the water to be quite so warm when you are trying to increase endurance. If you have healthy joints, be careful not to push yourself too far at first, and loosen up for a few minutes before you go in the pool. The stroke you intend to do will dictate the exercises you choose, although you need to do general flexibility exercises because swimming works all your muscles. Don't embark on a long swim without being in top physical condition, as you could be in big trouble if you start to run out of gas and are unable to get back to shore. This is obviously much less of a problem if you use a pool, and you probably should restrict your swimming to a pool until you are in excellent condition. (Swimming in pools also does not involve fighting currents and winds, so it is considerably easier to start with.) And, as always, never swim alone, no matter where you choose to swim.

If you have arthritis, starting with warm water exercises as well as land-based flexibility exercises can help you get back into swim shape. You may find that the crawl and backstroke are difficult if you have severe arthritis in the shoulder, and the breaststroke or sidestroke might be easier. Slowly increasing the number of laps you do and your speed can help you to improve overall fitness. If you are having difficulty, you can use a variety of flotation devices to help you, or a kickboard if the arthritis in your arms makes things too hard at first. You can even choose to simply walk in the water for exercise, as the resistance of the water increases the intensity of the workout without the pounding that regular walking can impart to your knees, hips, and back.

Bowling

Yes, you can injure yourself bowling if you are not careful. Many of you probably think that bowling is more of a recreational activity than a sport, but if you have ever pulled your back lifting that sixteen-pound ball, or felt your shoulder pop as you release, then you know what I am talking about. Although bowling may not be the most effective form of aerobic exercise, you can injure yourself quite seriously if you are not careful. Make sure to loosen up for about fifteen minutes before you go bowling, focusing on the lower back, neck, shoulders, and any other area of the body that you have a history of problems with. Don't choose a ball that's too heavy, and wear a wrist guard as needed to reduce the risk of injury, as wrist strains are quite common. If you notice discomfort in your back or shoulder, consider taking some time off. And finally, if you have arthritis of the hands, be certain that your fingers fit comfortably into the holes—if they are too tight, you can continuously traumatize the joint and cause swelling and pain.

Other Sports

Obviously, not every sport that anyone could participate in is covered in this chapter. When you choose to participate in any type of athletics, be it hockey, karate, or badminton, you are at risk for injury or for worsening the arthritis you already have. However, if you take all of the necessary precautions, you will give yourself the best opportunity to continue playing at the highest level and to enjoy your activity more as well. A regular exercise program that incorporates strength, flexibility, and aerobic fitness, with emphasis on problem areas, will enhance your ability to play at the highest level for many years to come.

Sex and Arthritis

No, sex is not a sport, but osteoarthritis can affect sexual function in a number of different ways. Arthritis can make sexual intercourse painful. In addition, some medications, such as narcotic painkillers and some of the antidepressants, can inhibit sexual function. Sexual intimacy is an important part of many relationships and you may be reluctant to discuss the problems that arthritis is causing. This can lead to additional stress and tension.

Talking to your partner about the difficulties you are having can go a long way toward reducing tension, and may help you to discover different positions that cause less pain. Doing stretching exercises prior to intercourse may help you to get more comfortable; taking pain relievers about thirty minutes prior to starting foreplay can help. Sexual activity can help to release endorphins, your body's natural painkillers, so you may actually notice that your pain decreases following intercourse. Sex should not stop just because you have arthritis, and some of the same techniques you are using to increase your activity level in other areas can allow you to get closer with your partner.

Step 5: Choose the Right Medication

If you need medication, choosing the best one for you can be difficult. At your pharmacy you see a seemingly limitless number of alternatives, from simple aspirin to "arthritis formulas" that claim to have some sort of advantage over their competitors. And you haven't even ventured down the first of the rows of alternative medications.

The most important rule for you to remember is to talk to your doctor before starting any medication, even if it is over the counter or "all-natural." You may find that you have a medical condition that puts you at risk for serious side effects of certain medications. For example, if you have diabetes and take glucosamine, your blood sugar could go up significantly. Or if you were taking prescription Motrin and decided to add over-the-counter Advil, you could significantly increase your risk of developing an ulcer because both drugs contain ibuprofen.

Most doctors will tell you that unless you have a history of kidney or liver disease, you should try acetaminophen first because it is generally very safe and well tolerated. Topical pain relievers are quite safe as well, and if you have limited joint involvement these should be considered early on. Over-the-counter NSAIDs can cause ulcers and may interact with other medications, so consult your doctor prior to starting them. You may be told that one of the new COX-2 inhibitors, which are less likely to have negative effects on the stomach and intestines, could be right for you.

Starting on a good multivitamin that includes vitamins C, D, and E should be part of your strategy. Glucosamine and chondroitin appear to be safe for those who do not have diabetes, and may make sense for you if you already have osteoarthritis. Talk with your health care provider before starting these or any other alternative medications.

Many of you may be reluctant to take medication for your arthritis. I have always told my patients that I would much rather they be comfortable and functioning normally on medication than miserable off medication. Whether you need to take medication on a regular basis or only prior to doing certain activities, the right medicine can help you to do more with less pain. Remember that medications can often serve as a bridge, allowing you to start exercising to improve joint flexibility and muscle strength, and eventually reducing pain and increasing your level of function. You may find that once you have started becoming more active and are able to do the things you need to do to help your arthritis, you no longer need to take the medication. Don't wait until you are so debilitated that you are using a wheelchair before you consider taking anything.

Step 6: Find the Right Doctor

With the ever-increasing specialization in medicine today, finding the right type of doctor can be confusing. Most people have a primary care physician who handles most of their medical needs. Three major subspecialties of doctors commonly take care of arthritis patients.

Rheumatologists

Rheumatology is the subspecialty of internal medicine that focuses on arthritis and related diseases, such as rheumatoid arthritis and osteoarthritis, lupus, and scleroderma. Rheumatologists spend an additional two to three years studying after residency to become board certified in their specialty. Osteoarthritis is one of the most common diseases that rheumatologists see in their offices, and they can offer the most up-to-date medical care for arthritis patients. Although rheumatologists usually do not do surgery, they can prescribe the medications that are typically used to treat osteoarthritis and give injections. They are also familiar with the types of physical therapy and other modalities used to help you if you suffer from one of the over one hundred varieties of arthritis.

Orthopedic Surgeons

Orthopedics is a surgical specialty dealing with the joints and muscles and the diseases related to them. Orthopedists train for five years after medical school. They perform arthroscopic and joint replacement surgeries for patients with osteoarthritis, give injections, and can recommend therapy techniques to treat arthritis and injuries to soft tissue, muscles, ligaments, and tendons. Many orthopedists have physical therapists in their offices to help with the treatment of their patients.

Physiatrists

Physiatrists are specialists in physical medicine and rehabilitation who have expertise in therapy techniques and other modalities. Physiatrists go through a four-year training process after medical school and are astute in devising rehabilitation plans for a multitude of ailments, including strokes and brain injuries, and for patients recovering from surgeries. Most commonly a physiatrist will help to coordinate your therapy after joint surgery.

There are two types of primary care doctors you are likely to see as well—especially with the ever-growing presence of HMOs, which often require you to see a primary care doctor for all of your needs who will refer you to a specialist when needed. Most patients with PPO insurance can go directly to a specialist as long as the doctor is within the plan's network of physicians. People covered by Medicare can go to any physician who is a provider (almost all doctors), unless they sign over their Medicare card and benefits to an HMO.

Internists

You might think of internists as the doctors who are fresh out of medical school and have started their internship in one of this country's fine teaching hospitals, but internists are something completely different and constitute the largest of all of the medical specialties. They are to adults what pediatricians are to children; they are the primary care physicians who specialize in taking care of adults. Most of you who have osteoarthritis will be diagnosed and treated by your internist, including recommending physical therapy, prescribing medications, and sending you to an appropriate specialist (such as a rheumatologist or orthopedist) if necessary.

Family Practitioners

When people refer to their physician as their generalist or family doctor, they are most likely thinking of their family practitioner. Family practitioners take care of adults and children, and in some places still deliver babies and perform surgery. In most metropolitan areas, family practitioners serve as primary care physicians and may be the first doctor you see for your osteoarthritis. They may prescribe medication or physical therapy, or may refer you to a specialist as necessary. In more rural areas where specialists are not as plentiful, your family practitioner may also do injections and even surgery.

Changes in medicine have altered the types of treatment that may be available to you. Limitations in access to certain specialists, restrictions of medications by insurance formularies, and limits on physical therapy benefits have caused patients to look for answers elsewhere. You remain your best advocate in winning your battle over osteoarthritis, as the more knowledge you have, the better equipped you are to work with your doctor in making the best decisions about your care.

Step 7: Put It All Together

No arthritis strategy is set in stone. You may find that you set your goals either too high or too low. You may think that you want to be able to run three to four miles a day, but later find out that isn't your cup of tea. You may discover that swimming or tennis is more your speed. Try not to beat yourself up too much; it's normal to have a change of heart after a couple of weeks. Just make sure you decide to stick with something.

Your goals may be easy—for example, trying to get back into golf after a five-year layoff, or preventing the ski injuries that you have seen in several of your friends. You might try three or four different sports before finding the one that you like and building a plan around it.

If you have questions, talk to your doctor, therapist, other friends with arthritis, or anyone else you trust. On top of the exercises and choosing the right doctor, don't forget the importance of healthy eating. If you are down or depressed, talk to someone and get help. Try to find something that you enjoy, and the rest will come a lot easier—but, as the old saying goes, nothing worth having isn't worth working for.

Final Thoughts

You have seen your parents, friends, and colleagues suffer with the pain and discomfort of osteoarthritis, or perhaps experienced it yourself. You have been told that arthritis is an inevitable part of aging, so no matter what you do you will almost certainly get it eventually. But you also hear stories about eighty-five-year-olds who run marathons or play tennis, and you wonder what their secret is. How are they able to avoid or tolerate arthritis when so many others can't?

I cannot guarantee that you can live a life free of pain and stiffness. No one can promise you that. There are no miracles, the claims of some products notwithstanding. But I think the plan I've outlined in this book gives you a good chance to prevent arthritis if you don't have it, or function at the highest level possible if you do. Knowledge is a very powerful weapon. *Playing Through Arthritis* gives you the information and skills you need to beat this overwhelming and previously unbeatable foe. You can win the war against osteoarthritis. With a little hard work and information, you can overcome this disease and live an active and fulfilling life.

Bibliography

Adams ME. Cartilage research and treatment of osteoarthritis. *Current Opinions in Rheumatology.* 1992;4:552–559.

Adams ME, et al. The role of viscosupplementation with Hylan G-F 20 (Synvisc) in the treatment of osteoarthritis of the knee: A Canadian multicenter trial comparing Hylan G-F 20 alone, Hylan G-F 20 with NSAID's and NSAID's alone. *Osteoarthritis and Cartilage.* 1995;3:213–226.

Altman RD, et al. Capsaicin cream 0.025% as monotherapy for osteoarthritis: A double-blind study. *Arthritis & Rheumatism.* 1994;23:25.

Altman RD, et al. Hyalgan study group: Intra-articular sodium hyaluronate (Hyalgan) in the treatment of patients with osteoarthritis of the knee: A randomized clinical trial. *Journal of Rheumatology.* 1998;25:2203–2212.

Anderson J, Felson DT. Factors associated with osteoarthritis of the knee in the First National Health and Nutrition Examination (HANES I). *American Journal of Epidemiology.* 1988;128:179–189.

Andrews JR, et al. *Preventive and Rehabilitative Exercises for the Shoulder and Elbow.* Birmingham, AL: American Sports Medicine Institute; 1997.

Arthritis Foundation. *Arthritis Foundation Arthritis Fact Sheet.*

Austin S. Double blinded evidence supports cetyl myristoleate. *The Quarterly Review of Natural Medicine.* 1997;315–316.

Bendich A. Biological functions of dietary carotenoids. *Annals of the New York Academy of Science.* 1993;691:61.

Bombardier C. Comparison of upper gastrointestinal toxicity of rofecoxib and naproxen in patients with rheumatoid arthritis. *New England Journal of Medicine.* 2000;343:1520–1528.

Bradley JD, et al. Comparison of an anti-inflammatory dose of ibuprofen, an analgesic dose of ibuprofen and acetaminophen in the treatment of patients with osteoarthritis of the knee. *New England Journal of Medicine.* 1991;325:87.

Bradley JD, et al. Treatment of knee osteoarthritis: Relationship of clinical features of joint inflammation to the response to a NSAID or pure analgesic. *Journal of Rheumatology.* 1992;19:1950.

Brandt KD, ed. *Osteoarthritis.* Rheumatology Clinics of North America. W. B. Saunders and Company; May 1999.

Brandt KD. Put some muscle in osteoarthritis. *Annals of Internal Medicine.* 1997;127:154.

Bressler D. *Free Yourself from Pain.* Simon and Schuster; 1979.

Brittberg M, et al. Treatment of deep cartilage defects in the knee with autologous chondrocyte transplantation. *New England Journal of Medicine.* 1994;331: 889.

Buchanan WW. Prediction of organ toxicity with anti-rheumatic therapy. In: Bellamy N, ed. *Prognosis in the Rheumatic Diseases*. Boston, MA: Kluwer Academic; 1991:403–450.

Burkhardt H, et al. Oxygen radicals as effectors of cartilage destruction. *Arthritis & Rheumatism*. 1986;29:379.

Catella-Lawson F. Cyclo-oxygenase inhibitors and the anti-platelet effects of aspirin. *New England Journal of Medicine*. 345;25:1809–1817.

CDC. Prevalence of disabilities and associated health conditions: United States, 1991–1992. *Journal of the American Medical Association*. 1994;272(22): 1735–1736.

Cicuttini FM, Baker JR, Spector TD. The association of obesity with osteoarthritis of the hand and knee: A twin study. *Journal of Rheumatology*. 1996; 23:1221–1226.

Cooper C, et al. Risk factors for the incidence and progression of radiographic knee osteoarthritis. *Arthritis & Rheumatism*. 2000;43(5):995–1000.

Cryer B, et al. COX-1 and COX-2 selectivity of widely used NSAID's. *American Journal of Medicine*. 1998;104:413–421.

Degner F, et al. *Clinical Therapeutics*. 2000;22:400–410.

Dexter PA. Joint exercises in elderly persons with symptomatic osteoarthritis of the hip or knee: Performance patterns, medical support, and the relationship between exercise and medical care. *Arthritis Care and Research*. 1992;5:36.

Diehl HW, et al. Cetyl myristoleate isolated from Swiss albino mice: An apparent protective agent against adjuvant arthritis in rats. *Journal of Pharmaceutical Sciences*. 1994;83:296–299.

DiNubile NA. Osteoarthritis: How to make exercise part of your treatment plan. *The Physician and Sportsmedicine*. 1997;25(7).

Di Padova, C. S-adenosylmethionine in the treatment of osteoarthritis: Review of clinical studies. *American Journal of Medicine*. 1987;83:60–65.

Ehsanullah RS. Prevention of gastroduodenal damage induced by non-steroidal anti-inflammatory drugs: controlled trial of ranitidine. *British Medical Journal*. 1988;83:1081–1084.

Ettinger WHJ, et al. A randomized trial comparing aerobic exercise and resistance exercise with a health education program in older adults with knee osteoarthritis: The Fitness Arthritis and Seniors Trial (FAST). *Journal of the American Medical Association*. 1997;277(1):25–31.

FDA Arthritis Advisory Committee, written resource of committee meeting 7.2.2001.

Felson DT. Weight and osteoarthritis. *Journal of Rheumatology*. 1995;43:7–9.

Felson DT, Anderson JJ, Naimark A, et al. Obesity and knee osteoarthritis: The Framingham study. *Annals of Internal Medicine*. 1988;109:18–24.

Felson DT, et al. Osteoarthritis: New insights. *Annals of Internal Medicine*. 2000;133(8):635–646.

Felson DT, et al. Weight loss reduces the risk for symptomatic knee osteoarthritis in women: The Framingham study. *Annals of Internal Medicine*. 1992;116(7): 598–599.

Felson DT, Zhang Y, Hannan MT, et al. Risk factors of the incident radiographic knee osteoarthritis in the elderly: The Framingham study. *Arthritis & Rheumatism*. 1997;40:728–733.

Fisher NM, et al. Muscle rehabilitation: Its effect on muscular and functional performance of patients with knee osteoarthritis. *Archives of Physical Medicine and Rehabilitation*. 1991;72:367.

Frei B. Reactive oxygen species and antioxidant vitamins: Mechanisms of action. *American Journal of Medicine*. 1997;suppl. 3A:5S.

Fried LP, Guralnik J. Disability in older adults: Evidence regarding significance, etiology, and risk. *Journal of the American Geriatric Society*. 1997;45:92–100.

Fries JF, et al. Toward an epidemiology of gastropathy associated with NSAID use. *Gastroenterology*. 1989;96:647–655.

Garcia-Rodriguez LA, et al. Risk of upper gastrointestinal bleeding and perforation associated with individual NSAID's. *Lancet*. 1994;343:769–772.

Gottlob CA, et al. Long-term cost effectiveness of total knee arthroplasty for the treatment of osteoarthritis. Paper presented at 63rd Annual Meeting of the American Academy of Orthopaedic Surgeons, Atlanta, GA, February 1996.

Grazi S, Costa M. *SAMe:The Safe and Natural Way to Combat Depression and Relieve the Pain of Osteoarthritis*. Prima Publishing; 1999.

Griffin MR, et al. NSAID use and increased risk for peptic ulcer disease in elderly persons. *Annals of Internal Medicine*. 1991;114:257.

Gupta VN, et al. Pharmacology of the gum resin of boswellia serrata. *Indian Drugs*. 1987;24:221–223.

Halliwell B. Antioxidants and human disease: A general introduction. *Nutritional Review*. 1997;55(suppl.):S44.

Hill J, et al. Failure of selenium-ACE to improve osteoarthritis. *British Journal of Rheumatology*. 1990;29(3):211–213.

Hochberg MC. Factors associated with osteoarthritis of the hand in males: Data from the Baltimore Longitudinal Study of Aging. *American Journal of Epidemiology*. 1991;134:1134–1141.

Hochberg MC, et al. Guidelines for the medical management of osteoarthritis, part II: Osteoarthritis of the knee. *Arthritis & Rheumatism*. 1995;38(11):1541–1546.

Hurley MV. Quadriceps weakness in osteoarthritis. *Current Opinions in Rheumatology*. 1998;10(3):246–250.

Hurley MV. The role of muscle weakness in the pathogenesis of osteoarthritis. *Rheumatic Disease Clinics of North America*. 1999;25(2):283–298.

Ike RW, et al. How aerobic exercise can help your arthritis patients. *Your Patient and Fitness*. 1990;3(3):5–8.

Jameson S, et al. Pain relief and selenium balance in patients with connective tissue disease and osteoarthritis: A double-blind selenium tocopherol study. *Nutritional Research Supplement*. 1985;1:391–397.

Kelly GS. Bromelain: A literature review and discussion of its therapeutic applications. *Alternative Medicine Review*. 1996;1:243–257.

Kelly WB, et al., eds. *Textbook of Rheumatology, 5th and 6th editions.* W. B. Saunders and Company; 1997, 2001.

Kikuzaki H, et al. Antioxidant effects of some ginger constituents. *Journal of Food and Science.* 1993;58:1407.

Kovar PA, et al. Supervised fitness walking in patients with osteoarthritis of the knee: A randomized, controlled trial. *Annals of Internal Medicine.* 1992; 116(7):529–534.

Kramer JM, et al. Dietary fish oil and olive oil supplementation in patients with rheumatoid arthritis: Clinical and immunologic effects. *Arthritis & Rheumatism.* 1990;33(6):810–820.

Kujala UM, Kettunen J, Paananen H, et al. Knee osteoarthritis in former runners, soccer players, weight lifters and shooters. *Arthritis & Rheumatism.* 1995; 4:539–546.

Lequesne M, et al. Guidelines for testing slow-acting and disease-modifying drugs in osteoarthritis. *Journal of Rheumatology.* 1994;21(suppl. 41):65.

Lorig KR, et al. Evidence suggesting that health education for self-management in patients with chronic arthritis has sustained health benefits while reducing health care costs. *Arthritis & Rheumatism.* 1993;36:439.

Lotz M, et al. Cytokine regulation of chondrocyte functions. *Journal of Rheumatology.* 1995;22:104–108.

Lund JP, et al. The pain-adaptation model: A discussion of the relationship between chronic musculoskeletal pain and motor activity. *Canadian Journal of Psychology and Pharmacology.* 1991;69:683–694.

Machtey I, et al. Tocopherol in osteoarthritis: A controlled pilot study. *Journal of the American Geriatric Society.* 1978;26:328.

Malehan H, et al. Prognosis of total hip replacement: Results from the National Register of Revised Failures 1979–1990 in Sweden: A ten year follow-up of 92,675 total hip replacements. Scientific exhibit presented at 61st Annual Meeting of the American Academy of Orthopaedic Surgeons, San Francisco, CA, February 1993.

Mattingly PC, et al. Zinc sulphate in rheumatoid arthritis. *Annals of Rheumatic Disease.* 1982;41:456–457.

McAlindon T, et al. Nutrition: risk factors for osteoarthritis. *Annals of Rheumatic Disease.* 1997;56:397.

McAlindon TE, et al. Glucosamine and chondroitin for treatment of osteoarthritis: A systematic quality assessment and meta-analysis. *Journal of the American Medical Association.* 2000;283:1469–1475.

McAlindon TE, Wilson PWF, Aliabadi Y, et al. Level of physical activity and the risk of radiographic and symptomatic knee osteoarthritis in the elderly: The Framingham study. *American Journal of Medicine.* 1999;106:151–157.

McKensie R. *Treat Your Own Back (4th edition).* Spinal Publishers, Inc; 1985.

McNeal RL. Aquatic therapy for patients with rheumatic disease. *Rheumatology Disease Clinics of North America.* 1990;16(4):915–943.

Merskey H. Psychological medicine, pain and musculoskeletal disorders. *Rheumatology Clinics of North America.* 1996;22(3):623–637.

Mindell E. *The MSM Miracle.* Keats; 1997.

Minor MA. Exercise in the treatment of osteoarthritis. *Rheumatic Disease Clinics of North America.* 1999;25(2):397–415.

Mitchell D. Clinical applications for a revolutionary new anti-inflammatory oil: Cetyl myristoleate. *Journal of the American Holistic Veterinary Medical Association.* 1997;16(3):20–21.

Moran MG. Psychological factors affecting pulmonary and rheumatologic diseases. *Psychosomatics.* 1991;31:377.

Moskowitz R. *Osteoarthritis Diagnosis and Management (2nd edition).* W. B. Saunders and Co; 1992.

Mueller-Fabender H, et al. Glucosamine sulfate compared to ibuprofen in osteoarthritis of the knee. *Osteoarthritis and Cartilage.* 1994;2:61–69.

National Research Council. *Diet and Health: Implications for Reducing Chronic Disease Risk.* National Academy Press; 1989.

Norden DK, et al. Prescribing exercise for osteoarthritis of the knee. *Journal of Musculoskeletal Medicine.* 1994;11(9):14–21.

O'Malley PG, et al. The value of screening for psychiatric disorders in rheumatology referrals. *Archives of Internal Medicine.* 1998;158:2357.

Panush RS, Holtz HA. Is exercise good or bad for arthritis in the elderly? *Southern Medical Journal.* 1994;87:S74–S78.

Perneger TV, et al. Risk of kidney failure associated with the use of acetaminophen, aspirin, and NSAID's. *New England Journal of Medicine.* 1994;331: 1675.

Peyron JG. Epidemiologic and etiologic approach of osteoarthritis. *Seminars in Arthritis and Rheumatism.* 1979;8:288–296.

Prevalence and impact of arthritis among women—United States, 1989–91. *Morbidity and Mortality Weekly Report.* 1995;44(17):331–335.

Rao CV, et al. Antioxidant activity of curcumin and related compounds: Lipid peroxide formation in experimental inflammation. *Cancer Research.* 1993;55:259.

Rauck RL, et al. Comparison of tramadol and acetaminophen with codeine for long-term pain management in elderly patients. *Current Concepts in Therapeutics and Research.* 1994;55:1417.

Recommendations for the medical management of osteoarthritis of the hip and knee: 2000 update. *Arthritis and Rheumatism.* 2000;43(9):1905–1915.

Reginster JY, et al. Long-term effects of glucosamine sulfate on osteoarthritis progression: a randomized, placebo-controlled trial. *Lancet.* 2001;357:251–256.

Saag K, et al. Rofecoxib, a new COX-2 inhibitor, shows sustained efficacy, comparable with other NSAID's: A 6-week and 1-year trial in patients with osteoarthritis. *Archives of Family Medicine.* 2000;9:1124–1134.

Safayhi H, et al. Boswellic acids: Novel, specific inhibitors of 5-lipoxygenase. *Journal of Pharmacology and Experimental Therapies.* 1992;261:1143–1146.

Schoenfeld P. Gastrointestinal safety profile of meloxicam: A meta-analysis and systematic review of randomized controlled trials. *American Journal of Medicine.* 1999;107(6A):48S–54S.

Schulick P. *Ginger: Common Spice and Wonder Drug.* Herbal Free Press; 1994.

Silverstein F, et al. Gastrointestinal toxicity with celecoxib vs nonsteroidal anti-inflammatory drugs for osteoarthritis and rheumatoid arthritis. *Journal of the American Medical Association.* 2000;284(10):1247–1255.

Simon LS. Viscosupplementation therapy with intra-articular hyaluronic acid: Fact or fantasy? *Rheumatology Disease Clinics of North America.* 1999;25(2): 345–358.

Singh GS. Epidemiology of NSAID induced gastrointestinal complications. *Journal of Rheumatology.* 1999;26(s56):18–24.

Singh GS. Gastrointestinal tract complications of non-steroidal anti-inflammatory drug treatment in rheumatoid arthritis. *Annals of Internal Medicine.* 1996; 156:1530–1536.

Singh GS, et al. SCORE: A simple self-assessment instrument to quantify the risk of serious NSAID-related GI complications in RA and OA. *Arthritis & Rheumatism.* 1998;41(suppl.):S75.

Slemenda C, et al. Quadriceps weakness and osteoarthritis of the knee. *Annals of Internal Medicine.* 1997;127:97.

Sowers MF, et al. Vitamins and arthritis: The roles of vitamins A, C, D, and E. *Rheumatology Clinics of North America.* 1999;25(2):315–332.

Srimal R, et al. Pharmacology of diferuloyl methane (curcumin): A NSAID. *Journal of Pharmacology.* 1973;25(6):447–452.

Srinivas L, et al. Turmerin: A water soluble antioxidant peptide from turmeric. *Archives of Biochemistry and Biophysics.* 1992;292(2):617–623.

Stoltz C, et al. Depression in the patient with rheumatologic disease. *Rheumatology Disease Clinics of North America.* 1999;25(3):687–702.

Tanveer E, Anastassiades TP. Glucosamine and chondroitin for treating symptoms of osteoarthritis: Evidence is widely touted but incomplete. *Journal of the American Medical Association.* 2000;283:1483–1484.

Tassman GC, et al. Evaluation of a plant proteolytic enzyme for the control of inflammation and pain. *Journal of Dental Medicine.* 1964;19:73–77.

Theodosakis J, et al. *The Arthritis Cure.* New York, NY: St. Martin's Griffin; 1997.

Travers RL, et al. Boron and arthritis: The results of a double-blind pilot study. *Journal of Nutritional Medicine.* 1990;1:127–132.

U.S. Department of Health and Human Services. *The Surgeon General's Report on Nutrition and Health.* GPO; 1988.

Van Baar ME, et al. The effectiveness of exercise therapy in patients with osteoarthritis of the hip or knee: A randomized clinical trial. *Journal of Rheumatology.* 1998;25(12):2432–2439.

Vetter G. Double-blind clinical trial of S-adenosylmethionine versus indomethacin in the treatment of osteoarthritis. *American Journal of Medicine.* 1987;83: 78–80.

Warner, T, et al. Nonsteroid drug selectivities for cyclo-oxygenase-1 rather than cyclo-oxygenase-2 are associated with human gastrointestinal toxicity: A full in vitro analysis. *Proceedings of the National Academy of Science.* 1999; 7563–7568.

Whitcomb DA, et al. Association of acetaminophen toxicity with fasting and ethanol use. *Journal of the American Medical Association.* 1994;272:1845.

Wobig M, et al. Viscosupplementation with Hylan G-F 20: A 26-week controlled trial for efficacy and safety in the osteoarthritic knee. *Clinical Therapeutics.* 1998;20:410–417.

Woessner MF, Gunja-Smith Z. Role of metalloproteinases in human osteoarthritis. *Journal of Rheumatology.* 1991;18:99–101.

Wolfe MM, et al. Gastrointestinal toxicity of nonsteroidal anti-inflammatory drugs. *New England Journal of Medicine.* 1999;340:1888–1899.

Websites

aaos.org/wordhtml/research/oa.htm

allsands.com

arthritis.org

clinicaltrials.gov/ct/gui/c/a1b/show/NCT00010790?order=1&JServSessionIdzone_ct=auvc8e4re1

fda.gov/ohrms/dockets/ac/01/briefing/3677b2_05_gi.doc

hopkins-arthritis.com

netfit.co.uk

quackwatch.com/01QuackeryRelatedTopics/DSH/glucosamine.html

wholehealthmd.com

Index

Abdominal muscles, 20, 42, 156
Abdul-Jabbar, Kareem, 151
Acetaminophen, 96–97, 101, 102,
    143, 147, 166
Acupuncture, 117, 130–31
Adderly, Brenda, 119
Advil, 96, 102, 104, 166
Aerobic exercise, 16, 154
    benefits of, 59
    bicycling and, 161
    choosing appropriate, 162–64
    high-impact, 50
    low-impact, 65
    skiing and, 155, 158
    types of, 59–65
African Americans, 4
Age
    arthritis and, 2, 4, 6
    bleeding ulcers and, 103
Alcohol use, 88, 91, 96, 97
Aleve, 102, 104
Alpha-linolenic acid, 75
Alternative therapies, 11, 12,
    115–35
    acupuncture, 117, 130–31
    boswellia, 125, 126–28
    bromelain, 128–29
    cetyl myristoleate, 124–25
    emu oil, 125
    Feldencritz, 132–33

general guidelines, 117–19
ginger, 125, 127–28
glucosamine and chondroitin
    (see Chondroitin;
    Glucosamine)
homeopathy, 134
magnet therapy, 131–32
manipulation, 133–34
massage (see Massage)
Rolfing, 132–33
sulfur compounds, 122–24
turmeric, 125, 126, 127–28
Alzheimer's disease, 126
American Journal of Medicine,
    123
Anemia, 92
Ankle circles, 25, 29
Ankles, 141
    basketball and, 151
    football and, 159
    skiing and, 158
    soccer and, 154
    softball and baseball and, 153
    sprains, 151, 154, 160
    strength exercises for, 51–53
    stretching exercises for, 29–30
    volleyball and, 160
    walking and jogging and, 143
Anterior cruciate ligament, 5, 155
Antidepressants, 93, 165

Antioxidants, 76–77
Arm crossover, 37, 153
Armstrong, Lance, 62
Arthritis. *See* Osteoarthritis;
    Rheumatoid arthritis
Arthritis Cure, The (Theodosakis
    et al.), 119
Arthritis Foundation, 67, 68, 93
Arthroscopy, 111–12, 150–51, 168
Aspirin, 98, 102, 104
ATP, 123
Austin, S., 125
Australian Aborigines, 125
Axid, 104

Back, 19. *See also* Lower back;
    Upper back
  bracing of, 110
  softball and baseball and, 153
  walking and jogging and, 143
Back arch, 44
Barometric pressure, 4, 10
Baseball, 39, 152–54
Basketball, 20, 49, 65, 150–52
Behind-the-back twist, 146
Bending foot grab, 157
Bengay, 97
Beta-carotene, 77
Bextra, 105
Bicycle kick, 43
Bicycling, 62–63, 161
Biofeedback, 91
Bioflavonoids, 75–76
Bleeding ulcers
  COX-2 inhibitors and, 105–7
  NSAIDs and, 103–5

Blood pressure, 13, 16, 70, 107
Blood thinners, 103, 127, 128, 129
Bone scans, 4
Bone spurs (osteophytes), 3, 4, 10,
    31
Boron, 79–80, 81
Boswellia, 125, 126–28
Bouchard's nodes, 10
Bowling, 165
Bracing, 110, 148, 154. *See also*
    Knees, bracing of
Bromelain, 128–29
Bruxisms, 87
Buttock muscles, 24
Buttocks tightening, 50

Caffeinated beverages, 90
Calcium, 79
Calcium crystals, 7, 10
Calcium deposits, 132
Caloric intake, 82–83
Cancer, 13, 74, 77
Capsaicin, 97–98
Carbohydrates, 82, 83, 84, 90
Cartilage, 4, 6, 8, 10, 112–13
  bioflavonoids and, 76
  composition of, 2–3
  COX-2 inhibitors and, 107
  Diacerein and, 108
  exercise and, 14, 15
  gender and, 7
  glucosamine and chondroitin
      and, 119–21
  hyaluronic acid and, 100
  jogging and, 143, 144
  liquid, 111

microdamage to, 5, 15, 143, 144
MSM and, 123
obesity and, 70
regrowth of, 12, 96, 107
skiing and, 155
stretching exercises and, 18
tennis and, 149
in therapy, 129
vitamin D and, 78–79
volleyball and, 160
Cataracts, 99
Catching the rain, 38
Cayenne pepper, 97
Celebrex, 105
Cervical spine, 30
Cetyl myristoleate, 124–25
Chair lower-back flexion, 21–22, 153
Chi, 130
Chicken collagen, 129
Chin-to-collarbone stretch (sterno stretch), 32, 153
Chiropractors, 133, 134
Cholesterol, 13, 70, 116
Chondroitin, 12, 101, 115, 118, 167
  actions and indications, 119–22
  studies of, 116–17
Clavicle, 32
CMC joint, first, 2, 110
CMO, 124–25
Coburn, James, 122
Codeine, 101
Cold, 109–10
Collagen, 3, 6, 78, 129
Collagenases, 3, 6, 108

Colon cancer, 77
Compounding pharmacists, 98
Corticosteroids, 99–100, 103
Cortisone injections, 99, 148
Coumadin, 103
Counseling, 93
COX-1, 105, 107
COX-2, 105
COX-2 inhibitors, 95, 124, 128, 166
  actions and indications, 105–8
  turmeric as, 126
Crossover hamstring pull, 25–26
Crystal disease, 7
Curcumin, 126. *See also* Turmeric
Cyclooxygenase, 102, 103, 105
Cytotec, 104–5

Darvocet, 101
Daypro, 104
Deep breathing exercises, 89
Degenerative joint disease, 1. *See also* Osteoarthritis
Depression, 13, 85, 86, 91–93, 130
Desk lift, 57
Desk wrist extension and flexion, 148
Diabetes, 4, 8, 99
  diet and, 81
  exercise and, 13
  glucosamine and chondroitin and, 121, 122, 166, 167
  nutrition and, 74
  weight and, 70
Diacerein, 108
Diagnosis of osteoarthritis, 8–11

Diclofenac, 104
Diehl, Harry, 124
Diet. *See* Nutrition
Dietary remedies, 125–29
Distal interphalangeal joint, 2
DMSO, 123
DNA insertion, 113
Double shoulder grab, 37–38, 153
Doxycyline, 109

Eicosapentaenoic acid, 75
Elastic bandages, 151
Elbow flexion, 56–57
Elbow grab, 38, 153
Elbows, 141
    softball and baseball and, 153–54
    strength exercises for, 56–57
    stretching exercises for, 39
    tennis and, 147–48
EMLA cream, 98
Emu oil, 125
Endorphins, 130, 166
Endoscopy, 106
Ergonomically designed chairs, 23
Eskimos, 74
Evening primrose oil, 75
Exercise, 5, 6–7, 11–12, 13–68
    aerobic (*see* Aerobic exercise)
    health benefits of, 13
    incorporating into strategy, 141–42
    to meet goals, 142–65
    number of Americans involved in, 1

as preventive and treatment, 14–17
    strength (*see* Strength exercises)
    stress relief and, 90
    stretching (*see* Stretching exercises)
    warm water, 16, 60, 65–68, 164
Eye closure, 33

Facet joint, 31
Family practitioners, 169
Fatigue, 88
Fats, 74, 82, 83, 84
Feet, 141
    basketball and, 151
    soccer and, 154
    strength exercises for, 51–53
    stretching exercises for, 29–30
    walking and jogging and, 143
Feldencritz, 132–33
Feldene, 104
Feverfew, 125
Fiber, 83
Fibrin, 128
Fibromyalgia, 131
Finger splays, 40
Finger stretch, 41
Fingers
    jammed, 160
    strength exercises for, 57–59
    stretching exercises for, 39–41
Fish, 74, 75, 79
Fist circles, 40
Flaxseed oil, 75
Flexall 454, 97
Fluid retention, 107

Food and Drug Administration
(FDA), 116, 117
Football, 159
Footwear
basketball, 151
football, 159
hiking, 144
skiing, 158
soccer, 154
softball and baseball, 153
walking and jogging, 143
Forward flexion, 146
Forward lunge, 46
Fox, Barry, 119
Free radicals, 76
Full neck circles, 33

Gamma-linolenic acid, 75
Garlic, 122
Gastrocnemius, 25
Gender and arthritis, 2, 4, 7
Gene therapy, 113
Genetic factors, 4, 6, 7
Ginger, 125, 127–28
Glucosamine, 12, 101, 115, 118,
166, 167
actions and indications, 119–22
studies on, 116–17
Glucose intolerance, 121
Goals
exercises for meeting, 142–65
setting, 138–39
Golf, 20, 39, 144–47
Gout, 4, 7
Green lipped mussels, 125
Guided imagery, 90

H2-blockers, 103–4, 105
Hahnemann, Samuel, 134
Hamstring pull, 25
crossover, 25–26
Hamstrings, 24, 161
Hand flip, 39
Hands, 141
bowling and, 165
strength exercises for, 57–59
stretching exercises for, 39–41
volleyball and, 160
Headaches, 34, 87
Head-hand push, 54
Head-Thera-Band push, 54
Head-wall push, 54
Heart disease, 116
aerobic exercise and, 59
COX-2 inhibitors and, 107
exercise and, 13
omega-3 fatty acids and, 74, 75
stress and, 87
vitamin E and, 77
weight and, 70
Heartburn, 101, 103
Heat, 109–10
Heating pads, 109
Heberdon's nodes, 10
Heel lift
sitting, 29
standing, 30
Helicobacter pylori, 107
Hepatitis, 129
Herbal remedies, 125–29
High-impact aerobics, 50
Hiking, 144, 149
Hip and arm extension, 44

Hip extension, 157
Hips, 2, 141
    basketball and, 151
    football and, 159
    in-line skating and, 162
    skiing and, 156
    soccer and, 154
    strength exercises for, 50–51
    stretching exercises for, 24–29
    tennis and, 149
    walking and jogging and, 143
Homeopathy, 134
Hot packs, 109
Hyalgan, 100
Hyaluronic acid (HA) injections,
    100–101

Ibuprofen, 96, 98, 102, 104, 166
Ice, 109, 148
Icy Hot, 97
Ideal body weight, 5, 69, 70–73,
    84, 147, 159
    benefits of, 70
    caloric intake and, 82–83
    determining, 71–72
Index press, 58–59
Indocin, 104
Inflammation, 1, 4, 10, 125–26
    antioxidants and, 76
    bioflavonoids and, 76
    boswellia and, 126
    cetyl myristoleate and, 124
    corticosteroids and, 99
    ginger and, 127
    omega-3 fatty acids and, 74–75
    saturated fats and, 83
    turmeric and, 126

Injections, 99–101
In-line skating, 162
Insurance, 131, 151, 168
Internists, 168–69

Jammed fingers, 160
Jogging, 49, 143–44
Joint flexibility exercises. *See*
    Stretching exercises
Joint replacement, 111, 112, 168
Joints, 2–4, 5, 6, 8
    exercise and, 14, 16
    lumps on, 10
    neck, 30–31
    obesity and, 6
    stretching exercises and, 18
Jordan, Michael, 150–51

Ketoprofen, 104
Kidney stones, 78
Kidneys
    acetaminophen and, 96, 97, 166
    COX-2 inhibitors and, 107
    NSAIDs and, 104
Kneeling leg curl, 156–57
Knees, 2, 141
    aerobics and, 163
    basketball and, 150–51, 152
    bicycling and, 63, 161
    bracing of, 110, 143, 144, 151,
        158, 162
    exercise and, 14–15
    football and, 159
    glucosamine and chondroitin
        and, 121–22
    golf and, 146
    hiking and, 144

hyaluronic acid and, 100–101
in-line skating and, 162
jogging and, 143
skiing and, 155, 156
soccer and, 154
softball and baseball and, 153
strength exercises for, 45–49
stretching exercises for, 24–29
tennis and, 149
volleyball and, 160, 161
Knee-to-chest pull, 20, 25
Knuckles, cracking, 40

Lateral epicondylitis, 147–48
Lateral neck pull, 32–33
Leg crossover, 21
Leg curl, 48
Leg curl with arm extension, 48
Leg elevation, 21
Leg lift, 42–43
  sitting, 51
Lescol, 116
Leukotrienes, 74
Lidocaine, 98, 99
Life energy, 134
Lifting, 23–24
Ligaments, 4
  bracing and, 110
  exercise and, 14, 16
  hip, 50
  in-line skating and, 162
  neck, 30
  obesity and, 70
  stretching exercises and, 18
  volleyball and, 160
Lipase, 125
Lipitor, 116

Liquid cartilage, 111
Liver, 116
  acetaminophen and, 96, 97, 166
  COX-2 inhibitors and, 107
  NSAIDs and, 104
Locked-hand neck flexion, 33
Los Angeles Lakers, ix
Lower back
  basketball and, 151
  bicycling and, 63
  bowling and, 165
  football and, 159
  golf and, 145, 146
  skiing and, 156
  strength exercises for, 41–45
  stretching exercises for, 18–24
  volleyball and, 160, 161
Low-impact aerobics, 65
Lumbar lift, 157
Lumbar roll, 23
Lumps on joints, 10
Lupus, 167
Lying butterfly, 27
Lying foot grab, 157
Lying hip abduction, 156
Lying (hip abductor) kick, 51
Lying quadriceps strengthener,
  43–44, 47
Lying quadriceps strengthener with
  arm extension, 44
Lying scissors stretch, 28
Lying thrust kick, 47–48

Mad cow disease, 129
Magnet therapy, 131–32
Mammograms and vitamin E
  intake, 79

Manipulation, 133–34
Manual toe and ankle stretch, 29
Marathon running, 144
Martial arts, 50
Massage, 90, 132–33
Matrix, 3
Medicare, 151, 168
Medication, 166–67. *See also*
    Alternative therapies;
    Traditional therapies
Meditation, 90
Meridians, 130, 131
Metalloproteinase inhibitors, 108
Metalloproteinases, 3, 6, 108,
    109
Methylsulfonylmethane. *See*
    MSM
Mevachor, 116
Microdamage to cartilage, 5, 15,
    143, 144
Mineral Ice, 97
Mini-pushup, 22
Minocin, 109
Miracle of MSM, The, 122
Misoprostol, 104–5
Mobic, 105
Model arthritis diet, 12, 81–84
Moguls, 158
Morphine, 101
Motrin, 96, 102, 104, 166
MRI, 4, 11, 132
MSM, 12, 115, 122–23
Multiple sclerosis, 8
Muscle spasms, 16, 132
Muscle strength and endurance
    exercises. *See* Strength
    exercises

Muscles, 4
    exercise and, 14, 16, 18
    hip, 50
    obesity and, 6, 70

Naprosyn, 98, 102, 104
Narcotic pain relievers, 101, 165
National Institutes of Health, 120,
    124
Native Americans, 97
Neck
    bowling and, 165
    football and, 159
    softball and baseball and, 153
    strength exercises for, 53–56
    stretching exercises for, 30–34
    tennis and, 149
    volleyball and, 160
Neck (cervical) extension, 32,
    153
Neck (cervical) rotation, 31–32,
    153
Nerve damage, 4, 8
Niacinamide. *See* Vitamin B_3
Nightshade foods, 75
Nonsteroidal anti-inflammatory
    drugs (NSAIDs), 74, 96, 128,
    166. *See also* COX-2
    inhibitors
    actions and indications, 102–5
    in creams and gels, 98
Nutrition, 11, 69–84
    bioflavonoids, 75–76
    model arthritis diet, 12, 81–84
    nightshade foods, 75
    omega-3 fatty acids (*see*
        Omega-3 fatty acids)

remedies from, 125–29
whole versus refined foods,
    73–74
Nuts, 74

Obesity, 4, 6–7, 12, 69, 70, 82,
    142
Olympics, 110
Omega-3 fatty acids, 74–75, 79,
    124
Omega-6 fatty acids, 75
O'Neal, Shaquille, 150
Orthopedic surgeons, 168
Orudis, 104
Osseous manipulation, 133–34
Osteoarthritis
    causes, 5–8
    cure likelihood, 112–13
    defined, 1
    diagnosis of, 8–11
    other terms for, 1, 2
    overview, 2–8
    prevention, 5–8
    risk factors for, 4
    symptoms of, 2, 3–5
    winning war against, 11–12
Osteopaths, 133
Osteophytes. *See* Bone spurs
Osteoporosis, 2, 13, 49, 99, 134
Overhead elbow extension, 57
Overhead stretch, 146
OxyContin, 101

Pacemakers, 132
Pain, 2, 3, 4, 142
    in diagnosis, 8, 9–10
    exercise and, 14–15, 16, 18

injections for, 99
    stress and, 86
Pain medications, 101–2
Palm press, 58
Pantothetic acid. *See* Vitamin B$_5$
Paraffin wax treatments, 109–10
Partial situp, 42
Pasteurization, 73, 74
Pauling, Linus, 76–77
Pelvic tilt, 20–21
Pepcid, 104
Percocet, 101
Peripheral vascular disease, 70
Personalized arthritis strategy,
    137–70
    exercises to meet goals,
        142–65
    incorporating exercise into,
        141–42
    making time, 139–40
    setting goals, 138–39
Physiatrists, 168
Physicians, 114
    alternative therapies and,
        122
    exercise programs and, 16
    types of, 167–69
Pillowcase arm circles, 35
Pineapple, 128
Placebo effect, 120
Posterior arm grab, 33–34
Posture, 23
Pravachol, 116
Prayer push, 41
Prednisone, 103
Pregnancy and vitamin A, 77
Procrastination, 89, 138–39

Prostaglandins, 108
  bromelain and, 128
  COX-2 inhibitors and, 105
  ginger and, 127
  NSAIDs and, 102, 103
  omega-3 fatty acids and, 74, 75
  selenium and, 79
Proteins, 82, 83, 84, 90
Pseudogout, 4, 7
Puppet elbow circles, 39
Pushups
  mini-, 22
  standing forward, 55–56
  standing sideways, 55

Quadriceps, 14–15, 24, 45, 46,
    49
  basketball and, 152
  bicycling and, 161
  skiing and, 156
  walking and jogging and, 143
Quadriceps pull, 26
*Quarterly Review of Natural
    Medicine*, 124

Racquetball, 49
Rain, predicting, 1, 4, 10
Range of motion exercises. *See*
    Stretching exercises
Recumbent bicycles, 63, 161
Refined foods, 73–74
Relafen, 102, 104
Reverse situp, 43
Rheumatoid arthritis, 8, 167
  boswellia and, 126
  ginger and, 128

MSM and, 123
  omega-3 fatty acids and, 75
  osteoarthritis confused with, 2
  tetracyclines and, 109
  vitamin B_5 and, 78
  zinc and, 80
Rheumatologists, 167–68
Risk factors for osteoarthritis, 4
Rolfing, 132–33
Rolling outer thigh (hip abductor)
    stretch, 26–27
Rooster mane injections. *See*
    Hyaluronic acid (HA)
    injections
Rotator cuff, 145, 149, 154
Rowing, 50
Rubber ball squeeze, 58, 148
Rubber band finger extension,
    148
Rutin, 128

SAM-e, 12, 115, 123–24
Saturated fats, 74, 83
Scleroderma, 167
Sea cucumber, 125
Selenium, 79, 81
Sex, 165–66
Shark cartilage, 129
Shoes. *See* Footwear
Shoulder extension and flexion,
    54–55
Shoulder grab
  double, 37–38, 153
  single, 37, 153
Shoulder shrug, 35, 153
Shoulder touch, 39

Shoulders
  bowling and, 165
  football and, 159
  golf and, 145, 146
  softball and baseball and, 153–54
  strength exercises for, 53–56
  stretching exercises for, 34–38
  tennis and, 149
  volleyball and, 160, 161
Side effects
  of acetaminophen, 96
  of alternative therapies, 118
  of boswellia, 126
  of cartilage and collagen therapy, 129
  of corticosteroids, 99–100
  of COX-2 inhibitors, 105–7
  of ginger, 127
  of NSAIDs, 103–5
  of tramadol, 101
Side (hip abductor) kick, 50–51
Side squat, 47
Single shoulder grab, 37, 153
Sitting arm butterfly, 36
Sitting butterfly, 26
Sitting heel lift, 29
Sitting leg lift, 51
Sitting shoulder flexion, 35–36
Sitting technique, 23
Situps
  partial, 42
  reverse, 43
Skiing, 49, 110, 155–59
Sleep, 90
Snowboarding, 155–59

Soccer, 49, 65, 154
Softball, 152–54
Solanine, 75
Sosa, Sammy, 153
Soybeans, 74
Spine, 2, 30, 133, 141
Sports
  exercises for, 142–65
  number of Americans involved in, 1
Sports Illustrated, 159
Stair climbing, 158
Stair lunge, 156
Standing forward pushup, 55–56
Standing heel lift (Achilles stretch), 30
Standing sideways pushup, 55
Standing straight-leg kick, 28
Standing waddle, 156
Sternocleidomastoid, 32
Stiffness, 8, 10
Straight-leg hip rotation, 28
Strength exercises, 16, 41–59
  aerobics and, 163
  for ankles and feet, 51–53
  basketball and, 152
  bicycling and, 161
  for elbows, 56–57
  football and, 159
  golf and, 145, 146
  for hips, 50–51
  in-line skating and, 162
  for knees, 45–49
  for lower back, 41–45
  for neck, upper back, and shoulders, 53–56

skiing and, 155, 156
soccer and, 154
softball and baseball and, 154
tennis and, 149
volleyball and, 160
for wrists, hands, and fingers,
    57–59
Stress, 85–91
Stretching exercises, 16, 17–41
aerobics and, 163
for ankles and feet, 29–30
basketball and, 152
bicycling and, 161
for elbows, 39
football and, 159
golf and, 145–46
for knees and hips, 24–29
for lower back, 18–24
for neck, 30–34
prior to sex, 166
skiing and, 155, 156
soccer and, 154
softball and baseball and, 153,
    154
swimming and, 164
tennis and, 149
for upper back and shoulders,
    34–38
volleyball and, 160
for wrists, hands, and fingers,
    39–41
Stroke, 13, 59, 70
Subchondral bone, 3, 78–79
Substance P, 97
Sulfur compounds, 122–24

Sumycin, 109
Support groups, 93
Surgery, 111–12, 148
Swaying neck extension, 33
Swelling, 3–4, 10
Swimming, 64, 67–68, 149,
    164
Swiss ball, 46, 47
Swiss ball side to side, 48–49
Symptoms of arthritis, 2, 3–5
Synovial fluid, 2, 15–16, 100
Synovium, 2, 3, 4
Synvisc, 100

Table quadriceps stretch, 27
Tagamet, 104
Tai chi, 63–64
Tendons, 4, 14, 18, 70
Tennis, 20, 39, 49, 65,
    147–50
Tennis elbow, 147–48
Tetracyclines, 109
Theodosakis, Jason, 119
Thera-Band, 49, 54
Thigh muscles, 24
Thumb grab, 41
Thumb press, 58
Thumb touch, 41
Thyroid problems, 92
Tight fist, 58
Tiptoe and heel stand, 52
Tiptoe and heel walk, 52
Tissue pickup, 53
TMJ, 87
Tobacco use, 88, 91

Toe curl, 52
Toe flexion, 29
Topical creams, 97–98
Traditional therapies, 11, 12,
    95–114
  acetaminophen (*see*
      Acetaminophen)
  bracing (*see* Bracing)
  COX-2 inhibitors (*see* COX-2
      inhibitors)
  Diacerein, 108
  heat and cold, 109–10
  injections, 99–101
  liquid cartilage, 111
  metalloproteinase inhibitors,
      108
  NSAIDs (*see* Nonsteroidal
      anti-inflammatory drugs)
  pain medications, 101–2
  surgery, 111–12, 148
  tetracyclines, 109
  topical creams, 97–98
Tramadol, 101
Trauma, 4, 5, 6
Treadmills, 61
Trypsin, 128
Turmeric, 125, 126, 127–28
Twinges and Hinges classes, 67
Tylenol. *See* Acetaminophen
Type II collagen, 129

Ulcers, 96, 101, 166. *See also*
    Bleeding ulcers
Ultracet, 101
Ultram, 101

Upper back
  strength exercises for, 53–56
  stretching exercises for, 34–38
Uric acid, 7

Varicose veins, 70
Vibramycin, 109
Vicodin, 101
Vioxx, 105
Viscosupplementation, 100
Vitamin A, 77, 81
Vitamin B (complex), 77–78
Vitamin B_3, 77, 81
Vitamin B_5, 77–78, 81
Vitamin C, 77, 78, 81, 167
Vitamin D, 77, 78–79, 81, 167
Vitamin E, 77, 79, 81, 167
Vitamins and minerals, 76–80, 81,
    167
Volleyball, 160–61
Voltaren, 102, 104

Waddle and pigeon-toed walk, 51
Walking, 60, 61–62, 141, 143–44,
    149
Walking the wall, 35
Wall lunge, 22, 153
Wall squat, 46–47
Warm water exercises, 16, 60,
    65–68, 164
Warming up, 65
Water hip abduction and flexion,
    66
Water jog, 66
Water kick, 67

Water two-legged hop, 67
Water windmills, 67
Wheat grains, 125
White willow bark, 125
Whole foods, 73–74
Windmills, 36
    water, 67
Women and arthritis, 2, 4, 7
Woods, Tiger, 145
Wrist circles, 40
Wrist flexion and extension, 58
Wrist glide, 40
Wrist guards, 165

Wrists, 141
    bowling and, 165
    golf and, 145, 146
    strength exercises for, 57–59
    stretching exercises for, 39–41

X-rays, 4, 11, 14

Yoga, 63–64, 91

Zantac, 104
Zinc, 80, 81
Zocor, 116